MIX
Papier aus verantwortungsvollen Quellen
Paper from responsible sources
FSC® C105338

Diana Bednarek

Entering successfull the Indian market

Recommendations and challenges for German small and medium-sized companies

Anchor Academic
Publishing

Bednarek, Diana: Entering successfull the Indian market: Recommendations and challenges for German small and medium-sized companies.
Hamburg, Anchor Academic Publishing 2013

Buch-ISBN: 978-3-95489-123-8
PDF-eBook-ISBN: 978-3-95489-623-3
Druck/Herstellung: Anchor Academic Publishing, Hamburg, 2013

Bibliografische Information der Deutschen Nationalbibliothek:
Die Deutsche Nationalbibliothek verzeichnet diese Publikation in der Deutschen Nationalbibliografie; detaillierte bibliografische Daten sind im Internet über http://dnb.d-nb.de abrufbar.

Bibliographical Information of the German National Library:
The German National Library lists this publication in the German National Bibliography. Detailed bibliographic data can be found at: http://dnb.d-nb.de

Contents

List of abbreviations

BIS	Bureau of Indian Standards
DGFT	Directorate General of Foreign Trade
EOU	Export Oriented Units
FDI	Foreign Direct Investment
FIPB	Foreign Investment Promotion Board
GDP	Gross Domestic Product
IMF	International Monetary Found
INR	Indian Rupee
IST	Indian Standard Time
MRP	Maximum Retail Price
PPP	Public Private Partnerships
PRO	Public Relation Officer
RBI	Reserve Bank of India
SEZ	Special Economic Zones
SME	Small and medium-sized enterprises
TRIPS	Agreement on Trade-related Aspects of Intellectual Property Rights
WTO	World Trade Organisation

1. Introduction

Freedom of the press and a reliable democracy, the demographic development with a youth and consumer-oriented middle class, increasing investments in education and infrastructure, an effective finance market with comparable low rates of non-performing loans as well as a dependable legal system are the foundation of India's economic revival within the last years and will ensure that this dynamic will continue. Therefore the foreign trade between Germany and India increased within the last years and German companies started their business in India. Entering new markets harbour different risks whereupon small and medium-sized companies are facing additional issues of less financial and human resources, absent experience abroad, the ignorance of the respective national language and costs for the international market development.

The expenditure of time for building up new businesses is often underestimated by German companies. In conjunction with the market entry, the requirements for sales, multitude bureaucratic pitfalls and the inexperience of employees are frequently misjudged. Therefore many companies indicate that two up to three years should be scheduled until a company is marketable. Initially, the profitability is hindered by high investments for infrastructure, human resources, transport, logistic and sales.[1] Companies operating in India should have enough power of endurance in regard of establishing business relationships and of being successful in the Indian market as frequently higher than expected expenses have to be spent in the first years.[2]

Within the literature market entry barriers are described whereupon analyzes for small and medium-sized companies have not been conducted. The most important market entry barriers for large concerns are the insufficient infrastructure, the high bureaucracy, the forbidden corruption, the antiquated caste system, the confusing import regulations, high tariffs and taxes, the insufficient skilled labour force as well as the Indian mentality and diversity. Within this study these impediments are analyzed to identify if they also affect small and medium-sized companies.

---

[1] Cf.: Germany Trade and Invest (2010), p. 16 et seq..
[2] Cf.: Rodewald, A. (2007), p. 79.

1.1. Problem description and objectives

The identification, analysis and evaluation of market entry barriers for German small and medium-sized companies in India are the objective of this study and will be developed within six chapters. Moreover, recommendations to minimize or overcome those barriers are provided.

Small and medium-sized companies are increasingly confronted with new issues, but also with chances due to the persistent internationalisation of the markets. New markets are not only entered to guarantee existing competitive advantages and to expand. Furthermore, companies can benefit from substantial incomes and synergy effects.

Entering new markets harbour different risks whereupon the market environment such as customers, products, competitors as well as fiscal and legal conditions needs to be analysed. In comparison to large concerns, small and medium-sized companies are facing issues of less financial and human resources, absent experience abroad, the ignorance of the respective national language and costs for the international market development. On the other hand, small and medium-sized companies are using individual manufacturing processes or design niche products to compete in international markets.

India is characterized by its huge complexity of different races, languages, caste and religions as well as of its ancient cultural and social history. Detailed knowledge about the Indian culture and market is required to increase the success when entering the Indian market. The provided overview of those conditions is necessary to understand the characteristics of the Indian market and to consider this knowledge in daily business operations.

The topic "market entry" is covered in numerous reference books and studies about the market entry in India can also be found. These studies are discussing the market entry of big companies such as of Siemens AG and Robert Bosch GmbH in India, but issues of small and medium-sized companies are neglected. This academic void is closed by this study with the help of the implementation of questionnaires and interviews. Based on these primary sources, market entry barriers for German small and medium-sized companies in India are identified as well as analyzed and recommendations to reduce or even overcome them are presented.

1.2. Scope of work

The first chapter is dedicated to the problem description, objectives and the scope of work.

In the second chapter the terms small and medium-sized companies as well as market entry barriers are defined. As no general accepted definition for both terms exists, both will be specified for this study. In addition, different forms of market entry barriers are categorized.

The third chapter analyzes the Indian market and its environment to provide a basis to understand the sources of existing market entry barriers.

Chapter four informs about information related to the choice of taking questionnaires, the structure as well as the interpretation of them. On this basis, interviews were conducted and analyzed to validate the information provided in the questionnaire. The presented findings are the basis for the evaluation of market entry barriers and offer recommendations to minimize or overcome them.

Within the first chapters the theoretical and informational basis for the main chapter is presented. Systematically, existing market entry barriers for German small and medium-sized companies in India are identified in the fifth chapter. Initially, impediments for large concern are named and explained according to the literature. Subsequently, the relevant market entry barriers for German small and medium-sized companies are described. This evaluation is based on results of the questionnaires and the conducted interviews. Concluding, the impediments for large concerns and small and medium-sized companies are compared. Additionally, suggestions to minimize or overcome market entry barriers as well as the key success factors and challenges are presented.

The results are compromised in the conclusion whereupon target achievements and prospects complete this study.

2. Terminologies

The relevant terminologies "small and medium-sized companies" and "market entry barriers" are defined in this chapter. A standardized definition for both terms does not exist thus the underlying comprehension of them will be specified for this study in this chapter. Additionally, a classification of market entry barriers is presented.

2.1. Definition of small and medium-sized companies

Günter Verheugen, member of the European Commission stated that "Micro, small and medium-sized enterprises (SMEs) are the engine of the European economy".[3] In 2005, 23 million small and medium-sized companies offer about 75 million jobs and represent 99 per cent of all companies in Europe.[4] In Germany, 99.3 per cent of the companies are small and medium-sized enterprises in 2009.[5] As various data about the number of German small and medium-sized companies in India exist and different sources have been compared, this amount is stated to be about 2,000.[6]

Companies can be characterized with the help of the firm's size (quantitative definition) or with the help of soft facts (qualitative definition).

The quantitative definition categorizes companies on the basis of the firm's size whereupon quantitative parameters such as annual work unit and annual turnover are often used. Due to the fact that diverse institutions and economic regions take different magnitudes as a basis, the European Commission published a standardized definition[7] in 2003 which took effect on 1st January 2005 in countries of the European Union. According to this definition micro, small and medium-sized enterprises employ fewer than 250 persons and have an annual turnover of less than Euro 50 million, and / or an annual balance sheet total less than Euro 43 million.[8]

[3] See: European Commission (2005), p. 3.
[4] Cf.: European Commission (2005), p. 5.
[5] Cf.: Federal Offices (2009), s.p..
[6] Cf.: Weidlich, T. et al. (2011), p. 32.
[7] Cf.: Höhner, B. (2007), p. 18.
[8] Cf.: European Commission (2005), p. 2 et seqq..

Another widely used definition is given by the IfM Bonn, a research institute, determining small and medium-sized companies as enterprises with not more than 500 employees and an annual turnover of not more than Euro 50 million.[9]

On the other hand, small and medium-sized companies are also defined with the help of qualitative criteria. Important qualitative aspects characterizing small and medium-sized enterprises are the huge impact of the entrepreneur on the company, entrepreneur's personal contacts to its clients and distributors, concentration on individual customer requirements, flat organizational hierarchy levels, high flexibility, the company is not a subsidiary of a consolidated company and the company is less diversified.

The critical issue of qualitative approaches is the practical application as the mentioned data are hard to ascertain, especially for inquiries or even for a whole economic region.[10]

In this study the term "small and medium-sized enterprise" is determined as companies with less than 500 employees. The annual turnover is not considered due to the lack of information provided in the filled in and sent back questionnaires. The qualitative definition is not practical as detailed required information were not given by the respondents.

2.2. Market entry barriers

The entry into new markets is complicated because of different impediments which need to be analysed. High barriers protect established market actors and exacerbate that returns will be shared with new entrants.[11] An applied rule is that the higher the market entry barriers in a market, the lower the potential competitive constraints thus the likelihood of entering markets by new competitors decreases. From a macroeconomic view, the efficiency of competition is influenced by market entry barriers.[12] For example, a well-established company can be more competitive due to its economies of scale or stable customer relationships. New entrants have to spend more resources to advertise their products and might sell their products

9 Cf.: IfB Bonn (2011), s.p..
10 Cf.: Höhner, B. (2007), p. 20 et seqq..
11 Cf.: Freiling, J. / Reckenfelderbäumer, M. (2010), p. 162.
12 Cf.: Büter, C. (2010), p. 69.

for lower prices to attract new customers thus gaining fewer profits.[13] On the other hand, from a corporate-policy perspective, market entry barriers can be connected to particular business strategies. Companies can pursue strategies to overcome, reduce or build barriers to entry. The existence and intensity of market entry barriers are important decision criterion for the international market and location selection.[14]

2.2.1. Definition of market entry barriers

The discussion of how to determine the term "market entry barriers" started years ago and a general excepted definition is still not found.[15]
The concept of "market entry barriers" hearkens back to Joe Bain in 1956 with the definition "advantages of established sellers in an industry over potential entrant sellers".[16] On this basis, numerous definitions were developed and can be found in the economic literature.

The definition is simplified with the slit of the term into its components "market entry" and "market barriers". In this study, market entry is understood as the first engagement of a company in a foreign market. Market barriers are all factors that deter a company to entry a market (market entry barriers) or to exit from an existing market (market exit barriers). Building on that, market entry barriers are defined as the entirety of all requirements that needs to be fulfilled for a successful entry into a new market in this study.[17]

As this is a wide-ranging definition, the following part is dedicated to a classification of market entry barriers into tariff, non-tariff, market-related and company-related barriers. In the fifth chapter, these impediments are analysed as well as proofed if and to which extend they have an impact on German small and medium-sized companies in India.

---

[13] Cf.: Hitt, M. A. et al. (2010), p. 192.
[14] Cf.: Büter, C. (2010), p. 69.
[15] Cf.: OECD (2007a), p. 1.
[16] See: Bain, J. S. (1956), p. 3.
[17] Cf.: Berndt, R. et al. (2010), p. 108.

2.2.2. Classification of market entry barriers

Market entry barriers in the host country can emerge from legal restrictions, political risks, social and ideological reasons, lack of suitable business partners as well as from environmental conditions such as climate and insufficient infrastructure.[18]

In this study, a classification of barriers was created to provide an overview of potential impediments. With the help of this classification, market entry barriers are distinguished between tariff, non-tariff, market-related and company-related entry barriers.

Classification of market entry barriers

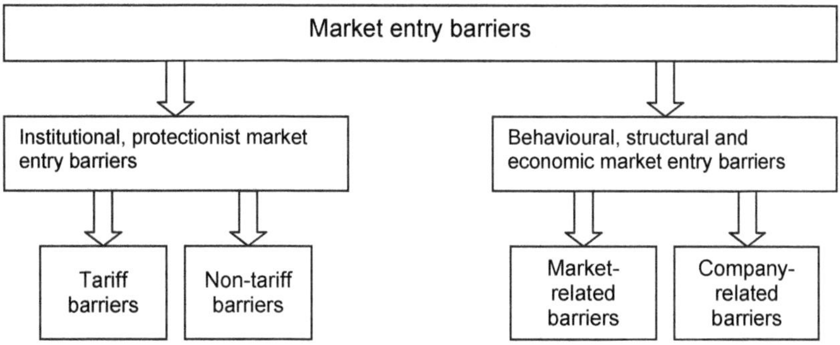

Figure 1) Source: Own representation

Tariff and non-tariff barriers are understood as institutional, protectionist impediments defending the domestic economy or specific economic sectors.[19]

In this study, tariff barriers result from all issues in relation of the payment of taxes, custom duties and charges. Non-tariff barriers can arise from embargos, import quotas, self-restrictions and administrative trade barriers in the form of bureaucratic prescriptions and formalities. In this study, non-tariff barriers are defined as all impediments arising from legal, non-financial regulations.

Behavioural market entry barriers are connected with the decision-maker in a company and can follow from deficient international experience, insufficient

[18] Cf.: Dülfer, E. (1999), p. 111.
[19] Cf.: Eschlbeck, D. (2006), p. 583.

knowledge of foreign languages as well as from cultural and mental distances to the foreign country.[20]

In this study market-related barriers are determined as all non-governmental constraints resulting from conditions which are unswayable by an individual company for example infrastructure and environment.

Company-related barriers are caused by interior structures of a company whereupon basic knowledge about the host country or about market conditions such as the competitive environment and customer needs are often ignored.[21]

All non-governmental impediments which are influenceable by an individual company or which affect the daily business of a company are understood as company-related barriers in this study.

[20] Cf.: Büter, C. (2010), p. 70 et seqq..
[21] Cf.: Eschlbeck, D. (2006), p. 583.

3. Analysis of the market environment

In this part an overview of the Indian market environment is provided as these conditions are essential to understand the sources of market entry barriers arising for German companies operating in India. This objective is reached by dividing this section into economic, political and legal as well as into socio-cultural conditions.

3.1. Economic conditions

Despite of the Indian advancement in international top classes in sectors such as information technology, pharmacy, research in astronautics and biotechnology as well as its positive economic growth in the past years, India remains an emerging country. Presently, India is leading the world in low-cost and efficient electronic commerce services. The IT sector is the fastest growing branch, even in times of economic uncertainty.[22] Therefore India is a favoured country for outsourcing of call centres, labour intensive data synchronisation and further services as well as for Business Process Outsourcing.[23]

India's objective is to become an international recognized manufacturing and export platform as well as a sourcing centre for international operating companies.[24]

3.1.1. Economic reforms since 1991 and India's actual economic structure

After gaining their independency in 1947, India's economy was characterized by governmental intervention and isolation from international trade activities by the enforcement of high tariffs and quantitative restrictions.[25] After several years of closed economy, foreign exchange shortages and inefficient productions resulting in high budget deficits and increased inflation, India was confronted by a macroeconomic crisis.[26] As a consequence, India applied to the International Monetary Found (IMF) for credits and began to internationalize its economy by the implementation of extensive reforms as well as by the reduction of restrictions in 1991.[27] The crucial points of the reforms were related to industry, trade, foreign direct investments and technology.[28]

[22] Cf.: Todd, P. R. / Javalgi, R. G. (2007), p. 174.
[23] Cf.: Weidlich, T. et al. (2011), p. 79.
[24] Cf.: DE International (2011), p. 3.
[25] Cf.: Todd, P. R. / Javalgi, R. G. (2007), p. 174.
[26] Cf.: Agarwal, M. (2009), p. 1 et seqq..
[27] Cf.: Wiskot, G. (2009), p. 222.
[28] Cf.: Wamser, J. (2005), p. 41.

For the internationalization of markets the then in force licenses for goods have been mostly abolished, tariffs have been reduced from up to 400 per cent to on average 28 per cent in 2004, foreign direct investments have been permitted in many industries, embargos on imports have been shortened, state-owned monopolies in telecommunication, aviation and petrochemistry have been broken and the Indian rupee has been devalued.[29]

In spite of the economic reforms in 1991 India remains a controlled economy ranking on place 123 of 156 states on an international scale about the economic freedom of the Heritage Foundation & Wall Street Journals. The index is based on ten categories including trade policy, tax burden, state intervention, monetary policy, capital flows and foreign direct investments, banking industry, salaries and prices, property rights, degree of intervention and shadow economy. India's position in this ranking is reached because of the high trade restrictions, corruption, high tax burdens, high bureaucracy and governmental limitations.[30]

Nevertheless, India benefited from the economic reforms from 1991 onwards and high real GDP growth rates have been generated with an annually average of around 7 per cent in the period from 1997 to 2007.[31]

Until 1991, small and medium-sized companies did not compete with other companies worldwide. After the implementation of reforms, small and medium-sized companies were no longer protected by trade barriers and faced intensive competition thus they needed to improve their efficiencies and innovativeness.[32]

The Indian economy is still dominated by the informal sector consisting of micro and small business units with less than 20 employees.[33] 91.5 per cent of the work force is employed in these companies which are not officially registered and labour laws are not enacted. Moreover, pension funds and health insurance do not exist in this unorganized sector. On the contrary, in the organized sector labour laws are enforced and a minimum of social security is guaranteed.[34] The share on employment in the organized sector decreases due to the privatisation of state-owned enterprises.

---

[29] Cf.: Pilny, K. (2006), p. 39.
[30] Cf.: The Heritage Foundation (2012), p. 225 et seq..
[31] Cf.: OECD (2011), p. 192.
[32] Cf.: Todd, P. R. / Javalgi, R. G. (2007), p. 174.
[33] Cf.: Wiskot, G. (2009), p. 226.
[34] Cf.: Ossola-Haring, C. / Ruh, W. (2008), p. 89.

One of the main characteristics of the Indian economy is the disparity between GDP and share in employment in the agriculture and service sector as well as a comparable insignificance of the manufacturing industry.[35] A contributing factor of this development is the fact that India is a work-sharing society due to the caste system in which several economic functions were performed by specialized castes.[36]

The GDP of agriculture continuously depreciated in the recent years representing 16.2 per cent in 2010.[37] The main concern of the Indian government remains the agriculture as 52 per cent of the working population directly depends on this sector. This situation is worsened by the grave scarcity of capital, undersized cultivated areas and stagnated crops as well as by absent distribution channels.[38]

On the opposite, India's wealth and growth is dominated by the service sector generating a GDP of 55.4 per cent in 2010[39] whereupon just 25 per cent of the working population are employed in this sector. Companies operating in the service sector were successful in the market positioning with the help of modern communication technology and low capital investments as well as with sufficient human resources and know how. [40]

On the other hand, the GDP of the manufacturing industry is stagnating[41] and reached 28.4 per cent in 2010. From a governmental point of view, India's poverty can be vanquished by an employment creation, especially for unqualified and low-skilled workers, in the manufacturing industry. The development of the manufacturing industry is hindered due to the lack of capital, an insufficient infrastructure and numerous legal regulations.[42]

Even though, the Indian service sector succeed in the last years, the competitive situation is changing as for example call centre services are offered at lower prices from other Asian countries. Thus the production of the manufacturing industry needs to be promoted and further reforms for the reduction of bureaucracy, taxes and tariffs should be conducted.[43]

---

[35] Cf.: Handelskammer Hamburg (2010), s.p..
[36] Cf.: Pilny, K. (2006), p. 44.
[37] Cf.: Federal Offices (2011), p. 2.
[38] Cf.: Handelskammer Hamburg (2010), s.p..
[39] Cf.: Federal Offices (2011), p. 2.
[40] Cf.: Pilny, K. (2006), p. 45.
[41] Cf.: Handelskammer Hamburg (2010), s.p..
[42] Cf.: Federal Offices (2011), p. 2.
[43] Cf.: Chopin, C. (2009), p. 8.

The real GDP growth rate increased by 10.1 per cent in 2011 in comparison to 2010.[44] However, the boom is curbed and the real GDP growth rate depreciated in the first quarter of 2012, reaching seven to eight per cent. Especially, the expectations for the industry are worsened due to the uncertain development in important distribution regions like the United States of America and Europe. Additionally, the inflation accelerates driven by rising food prices, incomes and interest rates. The persistent inflation could not been lowered and remains high in the long run, even though the Reserve Bank of India increased the refinancing rate several times. Therefore the investors' confidence declines and less new projects are announced.[45]

Summarized, series of improvements, increasing India's economic growth and international attractiveness were caused by a multitude of Indian reforms. However, India is still facing various issues hindering economic growth and creation of investors' confidence thus further reforms are necessary.[46]

3.1.2. Foreign Direct Investment (FDI) and German-Indian relationship

Nowadays, Foreign Direct Investments (FDI's) are possible in almost all sectors except agriculture, retail training and atomic energy. Sectors with the highest foreign investments are IT, electronic, services, transport industry and energy.[47]
FDI's can be accomplished either under automatic route or under governmental approval. Under automatic route FDI's up to 100 per cent are legal without previous approval by the government or the Reserve Bank of India (RBI).[48] For specific sectors such as telecommunication, mining, insurance, retail industry and defence approvals by the Foreign Investment Promotion Board (FIPB) are necessary.[49] Since 1991, FDI's enlarged from around USD 1.7 billion to over USD 76 billion in 2007.[50]

About 80 per cent of the German investors doing businesses in India are companies operating in the manufacturing industry. The majority is working in the automo-

[44] Cf.: Federal Offices (2011), p. 2.
[45] Cf.: Germany Trade & Invest (2011), p. 4 et seqq..
[46] Cf.: Wamser, J. (2005), p. 63.
[47] Cf.: DE International (2011), p. 6.
[48] Cf.: Ministry of Commerce & Industry (2008), s.p..
[49] Cf.: DE International (2011), p. 3.
[50] Cf.: Indo-German Chamber of Commerce (2011), p. 1.

tive supplier industry, followed by the electrical industry, engineering and the chemical industry.[51] German conglomerates are nearly completely represented with an own place of production in India. In contrast, middle class companies are more hesitant whereupon their activities are rising.[52]
The foreign trade between Germany and India boosted within the last years whereupon Germany is India's largest trading partner in Europe and the fifth biggest trading partner in the world.[53] In 2011, German imports to India increased by 20.2 per cent in comparison to 2010, reaching Euro 7.5 billion. German exports from India rose by 17.1 per cent to reach Euro 10.87 billion in 2011.[54] Thus the Indo-German bilateral trade has registered an increase of 18.36 per cent to reach Euro 18.37 billion.[55]

Moreover, India is one of Germany's major partner countries in regard of development cooperation and was supported by Euro 72 million in 2008. Especially projects in the fields of sustainable economic development, energy production and environmental policy are supported, mostly with the assistance of projects in Public Private Partnerships (PPP).[56]

The German and the Indian governments strive for bringing German investors to India; especially the German middle class should be encouraged to engage in India. Health care, biotechnology, aerospace and a more environment-friendly coal industry are defined as the new sectors of intensive cooperation.[57]

3.2. Political and legal conditions

The republic India is characterized by its stable parliamentary democracy for more than 60 years.[58] India is a union consisting of 28 federal states and seven union-territories with New Delhi as its capital city.[59]

---

[51] Cf.: Waldkirch, K. (2006), p. 76.
[52] Cf.: Wiskot, G. (2009), p. 68.
[53] Cf.: Embassy of India (2012), s.p..
[54] Cf.: Germany Trade & Invest (2012), p. 3.
[55] Cf.: Embassy of India (2012), s.p..
[56] Cf.: Wiskot, G. (2009), p. 59.
[57] Cf.: Waldkirch, K. (2006), p. 76.
[58] Cf.: Kirch, S. (2003), p. 6.
[59] Cf.: Rodewald, A. (2007), p. 31.

India is a secular democracy India and is marked by the freedom of religion as a constitutional right and India is generally characterized by its religious peaceful co-existence.[60]

The federal states are autonomic to a large extent as they are responsible for diverse reforms, education and health. In various federal states different regulations are in effect in regard of taxes, custom duties, religious prescriptions, alcohol and so one thus crossing of frontiers can result in unexpected border controls.[61]

As a former British colony, the British law, in particular the Common-Law-Tradition has a huge impact on India. Especially the business and the corporate law are comparable to the British, even though an independent development can be recognized.[62]

However, the Indian court system is complicated and in particular slow due to the persistent capacity overload. In addition, foreign judgments are often disclaimed thus foreign investors attempt to clarify conflicts in front of foreign arbitration courts. In principle, the free choice of law and arbitration clauses is accepted whereupon arbitration proceedings can last between one and three years.[63]

The Indian contract law complies with the Payroll Evidence Rule thus the whole tenor should be written down when contracts are designed otherwise important terms of contracts are not stipulated. For instance, this should be considered in regard of the discretion about trade secrets which are not automatically protected by the Indian law.[64] A signed contract is occasionally seen as a description of a current state and can be discussed if conditions are changing. In general, Indian business partners abide by contracts and the risk of litigation is comparable to other Asian countries.[65]

In the conflict with Pakistan about the Indian federal states Jammu and Kashmir in the northern Himalaya which is claimed by both states, the so-called Line of Control between Pakistan and India is unacknowledged by both governments as a border

---

[60] Cf.: Das, A. K. et al. (2007), p. 96 et seq..
[61] Cf.: Wiskot, G. (2009), p. 22.
[62] Cf.: Schaffer, R. et al. (2009), p. 77.
[63] Cf.: Weidlich, T. et al. (2011), p. 18.
[64] Cf.: Holtbrugge, D. / Friedmann, C. B. (2011), p. 117.
[65] Cf.: Weidlich, T. et al. (2011), p. 122.

but accepted as a zone of ceasefire.[66] These conflicts led to numerous terrorist attacks especially in metropolis such as in New Delhi and Mumbai whereupon several hundreds Indians died.[67] In 2010, rebellions claimed more than 100 deaths in Kashmir. In spite of interventions of the United Nations a lasting conflict resolution could not been implemented resulting in more than 60 years of enduring conflicts and three Indian-Pakistan wars. Peace processes are required to increase the Indian domestic and international security.[68]

3.3. Socio-cultural conditions

India with a population of 1.170.900 million inhabitants[69] possesses a vast cultural as well as religious diversity and a linguistic variety with Hindi and English as national languages besides 21 further constitutionally recognized languages.[70] English is spoken by ten per cent and Hindi by 36 per cent of the Indians thus the communication between people from different federal states is complicated. Nevertheless, English is the official language of the economy and is taught in universities.[71]

Cultural aspects profoundly influence a plenty of organizational, social, religious as well as familiar facets in India. Normally, hierarchies are fixed and lines of activities are clearly defined. Thus employees handle according to their duties whereupon inter-divisional requirements are often disregarded.[72] On the other hand, the impact on cultural system is decreasing due to economic reforms, modern communication technologies and the globalization.[73]

India is dominated by eight different religions whereupon the Hinduism is the most popular with a share of about 80 per cent.[74] The Hinduism is characterized by the caste system and dominates the Indian social order. According to the Hinduism each person belongs to a specific caste whereupon the affiliation is inherent and unchangeable. Thus the social status of each Indian depends on the appropriate

66 Cf.: Rodewald, A. (2007), p. 33.
67 Cf.: Tandler, A. (2011), p. 1 et seqq..
68 Cf.: Gorawantschy, B. / Suermann, F. (2010), p. 1.
69 Cf.: Federal Offices (2011), p. 3.
70 Cf.: Handelskammer Hamburg (2010), s.p..
71 Cf.: Wiskot, G. (2009), p. 29 et seq..
72 Cf.: Germany Trade and Invest (2010), p. 11.
73 Cf.: Davis, H. J. D. et al. (2006), p. 19.
74 Cf.: Rodewald, A. (2007), p. 38.

caste whereupon each area of life is affected.[75] Their current personality is a result of previous behaviours and thus fewer exertions are concentrated on improving one's present situation. Additionally, a collective goal of a family is often more important than individual objectives.[76]

In general, members of lower castes are economically worse off than people of upper castes due to their bad educational level. Nowadays, the government assigns places in educational institutions to members of scheduled castes and tribes whereupon these people are exempt from tuition fees.[77]

Even though the caste system is officially prohibited, the influence is still appreciable, especially in rural areas. However, the market-oriented economic policy will minimize the influence of the caste system whilst professions, incomes as well as social statuses will define the social prestige in the long term.[78] Especially, young people progressively replace the caste system with individualism and materialism.[79]

Despite of the impressive economic growth India remains a developing nation. Nowadays, 28 per cent of the population are living below the breadline with less than one Dollar per day and more than 50 per cent are living with less than two Dollars per day. Due to the huge share on the underclass, India is ranking on place 132 of 177 recorded states in the living standard index of the United Nation.[80] Millions of adolescent are obliged to do child labour to have one meal per day thus 25 per cent of school-age children are not able to go to school,[81] even though the employment of children under the age of 14 years is prohibited by the Indian constitution.[82]

The prosperity gap between poor and rich people is rising and poses a challenge as the wealth needs to be evenly spread to prevent an ordeal in India.[83] Without continuously high expansion rates and investments India is not able to get rid of its poverty and backwardness.[84]

---

[75] Cf.: Wamser, J. (2005), p. 86 et seq..
[76] Cf.: Davis, H. J. D. et al. (2006), p. 35.
[77] Cf.: Wiskot, G. (2009), p. 105.
[78] Cf.: Wamser, J. (2005), p. 86 et seq..
[79] Cf.: Müller, O. (2006), p. 21.
[80] Cf.: Handelskammer Hamburg (2010), s.p..
[81] Cf.: Ihlau, O. (2008), p. 77.
[82] Cf.: OECD (2007b), p. 10 et seq..
[83] Cf.: Müller, O. (2006), p. 27.
[84] Cf.: Handelskammer Hamburg (2010), s.p..

India is attractive for investors due to the fact that the labour force is one of the youngest worldwide.[85] The population pyramid shows that more than 60 per cent of the population is younger than 30 years and more than 80 per cent of the population is younger than 45 years.[86] Moreover, five per cent of the citizens are older than 59 years and thus in the retirement age.[87]
Proportionally more people in the age between 15 and 59 years are living in cities whereas children up to 15 years and people older than 60 years are living on the countryside. This development underlines that the work seeking population are attracted by metropolis to earn money for their surviving families.[88] The income of the urban population is on average much higher than in rural areas thus the demand for brand, quality and consumption products is superior in metropolis.[89]

In respect of the qualification and employment situation the Indian labour market diverges whereupon the major part of employees is unqualified or low-skilled. Most of them are working in the primary sector and 70 per cent of the rural population are unemployed. On the other hand, India possesses a substantial amount of well-trained degree holders of grammar schools and universities. By now 380 universities and 1,500 research institutes generate 200,000 engineers, 300,000 technicians and 9,000 postgraduates per year.[90] However, many colleagues and universities that are not belonging to the top class educational institutions are not praxis-oriented. Thus the Indian society is split into a few qualified employees and many uneducated people.[91] Annually about 13 million person are entering the job market whereby countrywide just 2.5 million apprenticeship training positions are available per year.[92]
Public expenditures in the education system are lower than in other emerging countries whereupon investments would improve the primary and secondary education. Nevertheless, free and obligatory education for children aged between six and 14 years is a governmental effort.[93]

---

[85] Cf.: Ossola-Haring, C. / Ruh, W. (2008), p. 2.
[86] Cf.: Rodewald, A. (2007), p. 37.
[87] Cf.: Waldkirch, K. (2006), p. 22 et seq..
[88] Cf.: Rodewald, A. (2007), p. 37.
[89] Cf.: Ossola-Haring, C. / Ruh, W. (2008), p. 35.
[90] Cf.: Waldkirch, K. (2006), p. 24.
[91] Cf.: Pilny, K. (2006), p. 78.
[92] Cf.: Handelskammer Hamburg (2010), s.p..
[93] Cf.: OECD (2007b), p. 10 et seq..

The level of literacy varies regional and declines due to the urbanization. In modern federal states the share in illiterate is about zero whereas in poor federal states like in Bihar less than 50 per cent of the population are able to write or read. Furthermore, the labour market outcomes are affected by the bad educational capacities as finding a regular employment is more difficult for illiterate people.[94]

On the contrary, India's economy benefits from the second largest English speaking population worldwide and a plenty of non-residents have returned[95] bringing their knowledge, experience and capital back to India.[96]

[94] Cf.: Pilny, K. (2006), p. 48.
[95] Cf.: Saini, D. S. (2011), p. 43.
[96] Cf.: Chacko, E. (2007), p. 131 et seqq..

4. Methodologies

In this chapter the methods to prepare the questionnaire and interviews are specified. This objective is reached by a description of the study preparation to elaborate the process of the enquiries. Finally, the analysis procedure of the questionnaires and interviews are described. In the appendixes the analysis and presentation of the results are presented.

For the processing of the research an approach consisting of a secondary data analysis and an own primary data collection with the help of questionnaires and interviews were conducted.

4.1. Quantitative and qualitative research methods

In relation to the main questions of this study a mixture of qualitative and quantitative research method was executed. For the questionnaire the quantitative research method was used whereupon for the interviews the qualitative research method was more practical. Subsequently the differences between quantitative and qualitative research method are provided.

Concurrently, the quantitative and qualitative research methods evolved into two independent domains of the empiric social research. Frequently in the quantitative research method, an ex ante advanced hypothesis is verified on the basis of selected data thus based on the theory the reality is analyzed and a theory is corroborated. On the other hand, in the qualitative research method priority is given to an open explorative question thus a theory is developed on the basis of the reality.[97]

In the quantitative research method, the question chronologies and the response options have to keep severely. Additionally, the conditions have to be equal for each interviewee. On the contrary, the qualitative research method tends to be more flexible with the interviewees by using a rough thematic guideline which individually conforms to the respective interviewee.[98] By using the qualitative research method a higher validity and deeper information content can be achieved, leading to a higher reliability and credibility of the results.

[97] Cf.: Lamnek, S. (2005), p. 118.

[98] Cf.: Flick, U. et al. (2007), p. 25.

Moreover, the communication between interviewer and interviewee as well as the selected sample are understood as two additional differences between these research methods. Interactions are completely neglected in the quantitative research method whereas these interactions are an important component of the research process of the qualitative research method.[99] In the quantitative research method the selected sample should be comparable to the population to ensure that the results of the sample can be translated into the population. In the qualitative research method the generalization of results needs to be explained.[100]

4.2. Methods of collecting data

In general, field researches can be accomplished by written, telephonic and personal enquiries.[101]

In this study questionnaires and interviews were chosen to collect data. This kind of method triangulation was implemented as required information for complex research objects are provided by this method diversity and the validation of the findings are eased.[102] As personal enquiries were not applied for this study, further explanations are not presented in this chapter.

Written enquiries possess the disadvantages of a low return rate and a high hazard of misunderstandings as the posed questions can be understood wrong by the respondent or the answers can be misinterpreted by the questioner. On the other hand, the interviewer influence is inapplicable thus the respondent can reflect his answer without any pressure. Moreover, regional distances can be overcome and costs are reduced.[103]

Interviews can be distinguished into standardized and non-standardized interviews whereupon non-standardized interviews are separated into structured and unstructured interviews. For the data collection of this study, structured interviews were conducted. Within structured interviews the wording and the question chronology is not compulsory thus the individuality is increased, but the comparability of the data

---

[99] Cf.: Flick, U. (1995), p. 15.
[100] Cf.: Mayer, H. O. (2008), p. 41.
[101] Cf.: Hüttner, M. / Schwarting, U. (2002), p. 70.
[102] Cf.: Wamser, J. (2005), p. 17.
[103] Cf.: Hüttner, M. / Schwarting, U. (2002), p. 71 et seqq..

is complicated. Commonly an interview guideline is used to achieve better results.[104] Guided interviews fulfil the requirement of openness in relation of the qualitative research method as the chronology of questions can vary and interviewee explanations are allowed. However, the interviewer should prevent excessive descriptions as the collected data are difficult to compare and analyze.[105]
For the preparation of this study, field researches in the form of a questionnaire and interviews were conducted. In the following part, the relevant question types are presented to serve as a basis for the developed questionnaire and interviews.

4.3. Question types

In general, questions can be distinguished into closed and open questions. The formulation of closed questions requires that all potential replies are known, otherwise open questions are suitable. In open questions the respondent formulates the replies on his own whereupon statements are hard to compare with other thus the analysis is more complicated.[106]

Additionally, questions can be posed with the help of alternative questions which can be answered by "yes" or "no".

Within selective questions in the form of multiple-choice questions the respondents can choose their replies out of several given response options.[107] In this case, the quantity of response options is limited thus the questioner should be aware of all possible replies. Otherwise important aspects can be ignored and the results can be biased.[108] Predetermined questions can be formulated in such a way that one reply is reasonable or that multiple answers are allowed whereupon this option needs to be specified. If an exhausting enumeration of response options is not possible, a category "others" needs to be added. This kind of interrogative form is determined as half open questions or hybrid questions whereupon the respondent has to verbalize the respective replies like in open questions.[109]

[104] Cf.: Pepels, W. (2012), p. 243 et seq..
[105] Cf.: Mayer, H. O. (2008), p. 37 et seq..
[106] Cf.: Schumann, S. (2011), p. 59.
[107] Cf.: Pepels, W. (2012), p. 247.
[108] Cf.: Hüttner, M. / Schwarting, U. (2002), p. 106.
[109] Cf.: Mayer, H. O. (2008), p. 92.

In addition, questions can be created with the help of Likert scales whereupon they are classified as closed questions due to the predetermined quantity of response options. In questionnaires Likert scales are frequently used to measure latent variables like approaches and opinions. Generally, the objective of scales is to summarize different indicators in form of measures to quantify the extent of the analyzed dimension. These metric scales measure variates and the data can be interpreted with the help of the statistical indexes like the median and arithmetic average. Likert scales can be built up of odd or equal numbers of response options whereupon the benefit of equal numbers is that respondents have to decide for a positive or negative reply thus neutral replies are not possible.[110]

In the following part the implementation of the described question types in the questionnaire and interviews is described.

4.4. Designing and dispatching of the questionnaire

First of all, the concept and the underlying problem of this study were concretized and the scope of work defined. For obtaining more comprehension for the theme, numerous literatures about India have been read. After scrutinizing the existing literature, studies about market entry barriers for large concerns in India have been found, but this topic is neglected in regard of small and medium-sized companies. Thus the relevant market entry barriers for big companies were elaborated, compiled, brought in context with others and edited. On this basis a questionnaire to survey the relevance of the founded entry barriers for small and medium-sized companies was developed.

According to the in the literature mentioned market entry barriers the questionnaire was divided into the following parts: operation, labour market, business market, economic climate, infrastructure, costs, standard of life, general, market entry barriers and conclusion.

The first page was dedicated to a questionnaire introduction to ask and thank for replies and to affirm that all data are treated confidentially. This introduction is followed by a summary of company-related data to ensure that the respective

[110] Cf.: Reiger, H. / Haas, B. (2010), p. 65 et seq..

participant belongs to a small and medium-sized company with less than 500 employees. Additionally, contact details and the type of operation were requested. In the following six parts, questions were asked with the help of closed question in the form of ordinal-scaled Likert scales with four response options to ease the analysis and comparability. Thus the respondents had the possibility to go quickly through the first questions by ticking boxes and the aspects were assessed to break the respective evaluation down.

In the general part, questions concerning aspects to be successful in India, differences in regard of the market entry between large concerns and small and medium-sized enterprises as well as their benefits in comparison to big companies were posed in open questions. In addition, questions were posed with the help of alternative questions which could have been answered by "yes" or "no".
The subsequent part was dedicated to market entry barriers whereupon open and closed questions were asked to obtain detailed information. In this part, the participants were able to choose suitable responds out of predetermined answers as multiple answers were permitted. Moreover, own experiences in an additional field named "others" could have been added.
In the conclusion the respondents had the possibility to decide if they would invest in India again and state reasons. In addition, suggestions to the reasonable enterprise size to enter the Indian market were requested in the final question.
As the questionnaire was sent to German as well as to English speaking people, the German questionnaire was translated into English.
The developed questionnaire is attached in the appendix 1.

Initially, a pre-test of five sent questionnaires was executed to test if the questionnaire is well prepared. Within one week three filled in questionnaires were sent back and positive feedbacks were provided. Thus the questionnaire was sent via email to the remaining 812 companies in the period of 17th of November 2011 and 3rd of January 2012. Until 25th of February 2012, 70 answered questionnaires were returned whereupon 30 questionnaires were answered by companies with less than 250 employees, and totally 40 companies with less than 500 employees filled in and sent back the questionnaires. The remaining 30 answered questionnaires were sent back by companies with more than 500 employees and are not evaluable as small and medium-sized enterprises are defined as companies with less than 500 employees in this study thus 30 questionnaires had to be neglected. In total five per cent of the questionnaires were analyzable. Finally, the data were collected, analyzed and presented.

4.5. Practical implementation of interviews

As the objective of the study is to identify opinions and experiences of German small and medium-sized companies in India, interviews were conducted in addition to the used questionnaire. Thereby the hazard of misunderstanding responses given in the questionnaire was reduced as important questions were repeated and the interviewer enquired the correctness of the replies during the interview.

Companies with less than 500 employees agreeing to conduct interviews were invited for telephone interviews as they were too far away located from the interviewer.
Generally accepted results cannot be collected with the help of telephone interviews as every reaction depends on the subjective experience of each interviewee. As experiences and experiential opinions were recorded, the telephones interviews were suitable.

On the basis of the respective questionnaire, guided interviews were individually prepared for each interviewee as different questions arose due to the diverse replies given within the questionnaires. These questions were written down to serve as guidelines for the interviews. During the interviews the respective questions were asked in the form of open questions whereupon the order was aligned to the course of the conversation and questions were cancelled if the interviewees already respond to them. Memos were written down during the interview and the minutes where completed from the memory afterwards. The information provided by the consulted interviewee was compressed as a repetition word by word is not suitable for the subsequent analyse thus small talks were not included in the interview reports. These summarized data were sent to the respective interviewee to ensure that the data are valid. All participants confirmed the correctness of the data.

The multitude of interviewees insisted on the confidential treatment of the provided information therefore the interviews are chronologic numbered in the appendix whereupon the respective industry of each interviewee is highlighted. Interview relevant information such as the date, time, duration, interview partner as well as places of location, the enterprise size and the annual turnovers are specified above. Subsequently, the interview report based on the respectively prepared guideline is documented.

Totally, 14 interviews have been conducted for gathering information for this study. (Appendix 3)

4.6. Data analysis and quality criteria

The data analysis task is to sort, review, analyze and summarize data for the decision making process. For achieving this objective the data were edited by extracting individual information of the filled in questionnaires and the interview. In addition, this information needed to be summarized to give a review and to ensure that they can be processed to gain differentiated and additional insights. The manual data analysis is time-consuming and is just adopted for qualitative, non-standardized surveys with few samples.[111]

For replies to open questions suitable response categories were created to ease the allocation of individual responses and to make them countable. Subsequent to the data collection they were listed, counted, processed and interpreted.
Additionally, the responses to closed questions in the questionnaire were analysed. The result of the questionnaire is presented in the attached Appendix 2 whereupon charts were used to make them visible and comprehensible.
Consequently, the findings were compared with results of the existing secondary sources to ensure their validity.

Usually the accuracy of empiric measuring instruments is determined by the reliability and validity. A measuring instrument is reliable if the same results are realized when the measurements are repeated thus they have to be free from random sampling errors. Moreover, a measuring instrument is valid if the defined

[111] Cf.: Berekoven, L. et al. (2009), p. 187.

aspects are exactly measured thus the measurement is free from systematic errors.[112]

In this study the reliability was verified with the help of 14 conducted interviews whereupon the credibility of the statements were checked by scrutinizing the given replies. As the interview responds are consistent with the information provided in the questionnaires, the reliability of the data are given.

The validity of the findings is also granted as the results of the questionnaires and interviews are comparable to the information provided in the literature. Moreover, the interview reports were sent to the interviewees subsequent to the interview to ensure that the written down information are correct. As the interviewees confirm the correctness of the data, the content of this study is valid.

Another important quality criterion of the quantitative research method is the objectivity as results need to be analyzed independently of the researcher. The objectivity is enhanced by the avoidance of interactions between the researcher and the respondent and by the standardization of enquires.[113] In this study the objectivity is granted as the researcher did not influence the consulted companies and the provided information were analyzed without reservations.

A main problem area of this study is the searching and finding of relevant and valid data thus a realistic image of India was received by gathering various sources. Based on that, the expenditure of time for data mining is intensive and often disproportionate to the results. Additionally, an upward trend to the falsification of official data was noticed, especially social data are corrected if India comes off badly in international rankings.[114]

For the maximization of the results' informational value, an analysis of all items applying to the defined research criterions, the so-called population is preferable. This form of research is also known as a complete inventory count reflecting all relevant data in reality. Complete inventory counts are often impractical due to financial, temporal and organisational restrictions. Therefore analyses are often confined to parts of the population which is known as sampling. The selected items of the population shall represent all data by reducing the effort and by benefiting

[112] Cf.: Hüttner, M. / Schwarting, U. (2002), p. 13.
[113] Cf.: Berekoven, L. et al. (2009), p. 80.
[114] Cf.: Wamser, J. (2005), p. 15 et seq..

from cost savings. Regarding all research relevant criteria the sample is representative if the distribution of the sample equates the population and if the sample forms a reduced, but faithful image of the population.[115]

In this study the population is defined as the entity of German small and medium-sized companies with Indian business relationship. As no reliable statistical data about the number of small and medium-sized companies in India exist, this study assumes that this amount is about 2.000.[116] Within this study, the population is randomly deduced from the sample thus the received results are projected on the population. With the help of the chamber of foreign trade, the India Desk as well as the chamber of industry and commerce, 817 companies were selected as a sample. According to the mentioned organizations these companies have business relationships with India, but the enterprise size was not registered thus the questionnaire was sent via email to these companies.

In total, 40 questionnaires of small and medium-sized companies were analyzable. As the exact population is unknown the representativeness of the provided information within the study should be censored. Nevertheless, the findings represent the results presented in the literature thus the information are representative in large parts.

To sum up, in this study a written survey was executed with the help of questionnaires, moreover telephonic interviews were conducted. Both methods led to the cognition that the in the existing literature mentioned impediments are valid for large concerns as well as for small and medium-sized companies. In addition, small and medium-sized companies are impeded by further barriers which are presented in the fifth chapter.

[115] Cf.: Pepels, W. (2012), p. 219 et seq..
[116] Cf.: Weidlich, T. et al. (2011), p. 32.

5. Market entry barriers in India

According to the classification of market entry barriers presented in the second chapter, impediments are differentiated into tariff, non-tariff, market-related and company-related barriers in this study.

In this chapter the most commonly occurring market entry barriers for small and medium-sized companies are presented. For reaching this objective, initially impediments for large concerns are described according to the literature. Subsequently, the most important market entry barriers for small and medium-sized companies are identified with the help of the evaluation of the questionnaires and the conducted interviews. Moreover, impediments for large concerns and small and medium-sized companies are compared. Concluding, recommendations to minimize or overcome market entry barriers as well as key success factors and challenges are pointed out.

5.1. Tariff barriers

The Indian market is still characterized by its strong protectionism therefore trade-political measures tend to protect the domestic economy from foreign competitors by the implementation of tariffs.

Tariff market entry barriers result from institutional issues in relation of the payment of taxes, custom duties and charges as defined in the second chapter.

5.1.1. Tariff barriers for foreign investors in India

Tariff revenues serve as important public revenues thus the reduction of tariffs directly causes drastic revenue losses. Even though import tariffs have been reduced from an average of 71 per cent in 1991 to an average of 29 per cent in 2001, they remain high in an international comparison.

In numerous sectors the tariff system is profoundly complicated and intransparent as various regulations are in effect for diverse products and just for few products a consistent tariff rate is implemented. Different tariff rates, exceptions, additional rates and charges as well as special provisions are used for various products. Moreover, the level of tariff rates can differ for one product depending on the

purpose.[117] Actual tariff rates can be found in the Market Access Database (www.madb.europa.eu).[118]
Additionally, tariffs and extraordinary taxes differ depending on the federal state therefore border controls between several federal states are exercised. As trade between locations of one company is exempted from taxes, companies can avoid these taxes and tariffs by declaring the transport as intra-corporate.

The Indian tax system is complex and India is not a low-tax country.[119] A multitude of different tax types as well as tax rates exist and the tax system is permanently revised. These changes not only affect the tax system which is continuously adapted due to economic reforms, but also the amount of tax rates.[120]
In the last years remarkable revisions of the tax system were introduced which led to a rationalisation of the tax structure, the enlargement of the tax base, the reduction of import duties and company tax rates as well as the introduction of a standardized value added tax system and accordingly the partially elimination of the so-called "Inter-State-Sales Tax".[121]
Tax surcharges of five per cent are charged for technology imports in regard of research and development. Moreover, so-called service taxes of 10.3 per cent are levied for certain services.[122]
Indian-domiciled companies are subject to tax liabilities with their entire worldwide generated revenues whereupon the effective tax rate has been about 32.445 per cent since 1st of April 2011.
Reforms are conducted in the Indian taxation law whereupon the scheduled implementation of the New Direct Tax Code will renew the direct taxation by further tax reductions and the extension of the taxable bases. Until now, the new regulations are not realized.[123]

In addition to the direct taxation many indirect taxes are charged for specific transactions. Overall, charges levied from the government, federal states or at regional level are intransparent and result in significant administration effort. These

[117] Cf.: Wamser, J. (2005), p. 72 et seq..
[118] Cf.: Germany Trade and Invest (2010), p. 27.
[119] Cf.: Wiskot, G. (2009), p. 254.
[120] Cf.: Wamser, J. (2005), p. 349.
[121] Cf.: Ossola-Haring, C. / Ruh, W. (2008), p. 161 et seq..
[122] Cf.: Weidlich, T. et al. (2011), p. 137.
[123] Cf.: Germany Trade and Invest (2010), p. 118.

charges are partially not allowable whereupon tax burdens up to 30 per cent arise. A simplification of the indirect taxation is aspired by the Indian government by the replacement of the Income Tax Act, 1961 by the new Direct Tax Code which has been progressively implemented since 1st April 2012.[124] One major objective is the standardization of the value added tax, the so-called Goods and Service Tax (GST).[125] A general value added tax would ease the tax system, products would be handled independently of their origin and a homogeneous business market would be established as federal differences in sale taxes and additional taxes such as Octroi and Entry Tax would be abolished. Some federal states are not accepting a general value added tax due to revenue losses.[126]

Customs duties are levied for all kind of imports whereupon the respective amount depends on the type of the imported good and its classification is often complicated. In the last years, tariffs were severely reduced and average ten per cent for a plenty of goods. In addition, specific regulations exist for stocked imports whereupon the payment can be deferred until the goods are retailed.[127] Companies do not have to pay additional costs if products are stored not more than three to five days whereupon the duration depends on the respective federal state. Otherwise, demurrage charges are levied which can be immense whereupon these tariffs depend on the federal state and the conditions of the goods.[128] Moreover, so-called Octroi's have to be paid for imported goods in several cities and federal states (for example in Mumbai).[129]

In addition, foreign investors are confronted with foreign exchange risks and should read upon them to prevent resulting losses.[130] In relation with the Indian market this impediment is not especially mentioned in the literature.

Companies operating in the fields of electronic, software, biotechnology, research and development as well as infrastructure such as telecommunication and electricity generation enjoy tax privileges.[131] Besides centralized tax incentives, especially

[124] Cf.: Weidlich, T. et al. (2011), p. 128 et seqq.
[125] Cf.: Germany Trade and Invest (2010), p. 128.
[126] Cf.: Wamser, J. (2005), p. 7 et seq..
[127] Cf.: Weidlich, T. et al. (2011), p. 134.
[128] Cf.: Germany Trade and Invest (2010), p. 30.
[129] Cf.: Weidlich, T. et al. (2011), p. 134.
[130] Cf.: Pilny, K. (2006), p. 55.
[131] Cf.: Wiskot, G. (2009), p. 235.

economic backward federal states in the north-eastern part of India offer additional regional relieves.[132]

Moreover, India attracts foreign investors by tax incentives such as tax allowances in the so-called Special Economic Zones (SEZ). In these areas the fiscal treatments and foreign exchange policy is more transparent.[133] Moreover, companies operating in SEZ take the advantages of duty-free imports of capital goods, raw materials and spare parts, diverse tax exemptions and licence-free imports.[134] Diverse federal states handle these regulations different thus investors should read up on.[135]

In addition to the SEZ, so-called 100 per cent Export Oriented Units (EOU) were created. These companies enjoy the same tax advantages as companies in SEZ whereas they do not have to be located in SEZ. Although more than 3,600 EOU existed between 1991 and 2001, the economic impact was low. India's EOU and SEZ had a share in the total exports of 3.5 per cent. In comparison, China's SEZ accounts for 40 per cent in 2002. Therefore the expected far-reaching structural changes did not occur, more foreign investors were not attracted and more jobs were not generated.[136]

5.1.2. Tariff barriers for German small and medium-sized companies

40 small and medium-sized companies affirmed in the questionnaires that typical market entry barriers relate to India's legal framework. Most frequently import regulations and customs, followed by issues concerning the Indian tax system were named by the respondents.[137]

Within the questionnaires the consulted companies were asked about their satisfaction in relation to the Indian taxes and charges whereupon 52 per cent of the respondents stated that they were "dissatisfied" or "very dissatisfied". This result is underlined by the fact that six of 14 interviewed persons specified tariff barriers as impediments for their businesses in India. In this connection, high customs duties, the confusing and ever-changing tax and tariff system as well as high taxes were

[132] Cf.: Weidlich, T. et al. (2011), p. 137.
[133] Cf.: Wiskot, G. (2009), p. 235.
[134] Cf.: Weidlich, T. et al. (2011), p. 25.
[135] Cf.: Ossola-Haring, C. / Ruh, W. (2008), p. 14.
[136] Cf.: Wamser, J. (2005), p. 221.
[137] Cf.: Appendix 2, p. XLVI.

mentioned.[138] The managing director of a software company reported about the protection of domestic companies with the help of higher tariffs levied for foreign products.[139] On the other hand, one corporate consultant stated that the market entry barriers are low in this field and that customs duties are almost abolished as well as comparable with other member states of the World Trade Organisation (WTO).[140]

5.2. Non-tariff barriers

India is regarded as a business location with a huge potential for the future. However, this development is particularly impeded by a multitude of regulations, bureaucratic barriers and the inflexible labour law.[141]
Besides to high tariff barriers, a plenty of non-tariff barriers affect the Indian economy such as quantitative restrictions, import licensing, exhausting mandatory testing, certification for many products and complicated as well as tedious customs procedures.[142]

Non-tariff market entry barriers are understood as all impediments arising from legal, non-financial regulations in this study.

5.2.1. Impediments resulting from India's high bureaucracy

In general, bureaucratic barriers result from the unproductiveness of institutions, overlapping of competencies, nepotism, uncertain hierarchies, filling of important posts by unqualified employees, absent autonomy of the administration and the immense impact of the policy.[143]

The efficiency of institution is low due to complicated regulations which differ at federal and regional level and which lead to tedious decision making processes. More than 71 days have to be scheduled and eleven bureaucratic steps have to be overcome before a company can be set. With regard to import and export regulations, provision of operating licenses and implementation of commercial contracts

[138] Cf.: Appendix 3, Interview 1, p. LI; Interview 3, p. LIX; Interview 4, p. LXI; Interview 5, p. LXII et seq.; Interview 6, p. LXVII; Interview 9, p. LXXIV.
[139] Cf.: Appendix 3, Interview 9, p. LXXIV.
[140] Cf.: Appendix 3, Interview 2, p. LV.
[141] Cf.: Weidlich, T. et al. (2011), p. 17.
[142] Cf.: European Commission (2011), p. 5.
[143] Cf.: Wamser, J. (2005), p. 295 et seq..

India is substandard.[144] Additionally, the cooperation with banks is connected with huge bureaucratic efforts, long lead times and a multitude of documents have to be submitted. In addition, Indian banks are risk-averse and ask for bank guarantees of a foreign bank.[145] Thereof, small and medium-sized companies are affected as no or low transparency of the financial situation of them exists. Consequently, loans are seldom obtained by small and medium-sized companies due to the increased risk of non-performing assets.[146]
One result of the high bureaucracy is that a plenty of managerial time of a company has to be scheduled for the contact with authorities.[147]

In comparison with other Asian countries such as Japan or Singapore, India needs to improve its economy to be competitive worldwide. One of the major barriers for corporate activities is the high bureaucracy as a multitude of administrative procedures with partial coincided competencies and a high degree of intervention lead to significant delays for investment plans.[148] Further economic reforms are necessary but they require majorities which are difficult to obtain due to the separation of powers.[149] The slow implementation of reforms weakens the faith of foreign investors and the Indian economy due to the power of special interest groups intervening against reforms.[150] Especially bureaucratic barriers and financial shortages retard or even hinder the implementation of important projects.

5.2.2. Import regulations and permitted economic sectors for FDI's

In India established companies are protected by certain regulations such as the Industrial Licensing Regulation and Reservation of products which confine the entry of new market participants.[151] The strict import license system was almost abolished whereupon the Indian government implemented a multitude of non-tariff sanctions such as certification duties of the Bureau of Indian Standards (BIS), obligation of identification and health certificates. Import licenses are not required for about 9,000 goods like machineries, components, raw materials and many

[144] Cf.: Pilny, K. (2006), p. 55 et seqq..
[145] Cf.: Waldkirch, K. (2006), p. 107 et seq..
[146] Cf.: Das, K. (2007), p. 75.
[147] Cf.: Wamser, J. (2005), p. 400.
[148] Cf.: Weidlich, T. et al. (2011), p. 8.
[149] Cf.: Waldkirch, K. (2006), p. 37.
[150] Cf.: Wamser, J. (2005), p. 72.
[151] Cf.: Indira Gandhi National Open University (2006), p. 7.

more.[152] On the other hand, import licenses are necessary for several consumer goods as well as for canalised items such as petrol, crude oil, vegetable oil, chemical fertiliser as well as for rice and corns.[153] For the import or export of goods, a foreign trade registration, assigned by the Directorate General of Foreign Trade (DGFT), is mandatory for all companies. Moreover, certificates of up to 32 institutions are necessary to import a product. Nevertheless, the government intends to facilitate clearing formalities for export firms and enables the import of machinery for agricultural producers.[154] Therefore foreign investors should be read upon if import licenses are obligatory for their produced goods.[155]

Since 2002, in many economic sectors foreign direct investments have been permitted and the ceiling for foreign equity holdings have been expanded or even abolished. However, foreign direct investments are completely prohibited in few sectors such as the defence industry and the agriculture as well as in some handcraft sectors that are reserved for small scale industries and where industrial mass production is generally not allowed.[156] In general, the amount of sectors reserved for very small companies has been considerably reduced.[157]
Meanwhile, joint ventures with up to 51 per cent stocks are permitted for foreign investors in the retail industry for single brand retail by approval.[158] Barriers to entry in the form of food safety, animal and plant health regulations has been raised in the last years to protect the domestic producers of agricultural products from international competition and has led to additional impediments for foreign exporters.[159] Furthermore, strict restrictions for foreigners exist in the bank sector and insurance industry.[160]

Commercial licenses for the production has been reduced to industry that are reserved for state-owned companies and industries with strategic, social and environmental issues such as distillation and brewage of alcoholic drinks, cigarettes

[152] Cf.: IHK Würzburg-Schweinfurt (2011), p. 1.
[153] Cf.: Ossola-Haring, C. / Ruh, W. (2008), p. 217.
[154] Cf.: Wamser, J. (2005), p. 72.
[155] Cf.: Germany Trade and Invest (2010), p. 25.
[156] Cf.: Handelskammer Hamburg (2010), s.p..
[157] Cf.: OECD (2007b), p. 3.
[158] Cf.: Weidlich, T. et al. (2011), p. 20.
[159] Cf.: European Commission (2011), p. 16.
[160] Cf.: Handelskammer Hamburg (2010), s.p..

and cigars, electronic devices for aerospace and defence, blasting explosive, dangerous chemicals as well as medicine.[161]

Foreign direct investments in the property market are connected with restrictive requirements whereupon foreign investors can only acquire properties with the help of an Indian corporation if they are Indian non-residents. The assignment of properties and the verification of ownership structure are protracted and complicated as no land register exists. Construction projects require a plenty of approvals and agreement procedures are tedious.[162]

Furthermore, for the transportation of goods, road permits are mandatory for each transited federal states resulting in additional costs and high expenditures of time.[163]

The Indian economy would benefit from the reduction of barriers to foreign direct investments. For example, the entire allowance of foreign direct investments in the retail industry would upgrade the productivity and supply chain management and would minimize the high rate of waste of agricultural produce which would led to lower retail prices.[164]

5.2.3. Impediments resulting from the Indian law

International operating companies need to be informed about the legal system of the host country as the violation of existing laws lead to sanctions or legal disputes. The awareness of the practical right-generating effect in connection with the sense of justice is important and influences the abidance by contracts in the business life.[165]

German companies should consider that the Indian law system is based on the British Common Law when contracts are designed as fewer details are regulated by law. Therefore all eventualities should be regarded such as payment defaults.[166] In Germany, contract negotiations are completed by the binding contract signing.

161 Cf.: Ossola-Haring, C. / Ruh, W. (2008), p. 20.
162 Cf.: Weidlich, T. et al. (2011), p. 48 et seqq..
163 Cf.: Germany Trade and Invest (2010), p. 62.
164 Cf.: OECD (2007b), p. 7.
165 Cf.: Dülfer, E. (1999), p. 328 et seq..
166 Cf.: Mitterer, K. et al. (2006), p. 68.

On the other hand, Indians attach more importance to individual agreements than to contracts,[167] consequently they are often renegotiated due to the fact that these agreements are seen as a basis for a current project and not as a law.[168] In addition, investors should be aware of that the Indian legal order is one of the slowest worldwide and legal procedures that are sued to the Supreme Court can take up to 25 years.[169] Conflicts with contractual partners can be reduced by contract negotiations according to the international instead of the Indian law.[170]

Non-tariff barriers also result from limited laws to geographical jurisdictions whereupon intellectual property rights, particularly software copyright, piracy rates and copyright laws are affected.[171] As India is a member of the WTO intellectual properties are protected. The trademark law was modernized with the so-called Trade-Marks-Act in 1999. Accordingly individual brands can be registered and are protected for ten years whereupon this period can be extended. The enforcement of violation is fast and effective. Injunctions, searches and confiscation are possible and practical. The same applies for copyrights which were adapted to the international TRIPS standards in 1999. Patents are protected for twenty years whereas software products or services are not patentable.[172] In addition, the patent law is territorially regulated and thus not enforceable in other federal states.[173] Furthermore, protective or anti-dumping duties are imposed on imports if the offence is constituted. The government wants to prevent the distortion of trade and the subsequent damages for the domestic industry due to dumping.[174]

Despite of severe legal regulations India remains a country of plagiarising of merchandise and counterfeited products are manufactured due to the slack enforcement of regulations and the common corruption. Caught manufacturers and retailers often buy themselves off or delay processes.[175] The lack of privacy, security and liability still lead to concerns to transact businesses in the internet thus the government should protect e-commerce.[176]

---

[167] Cf.: Dülfer, E. (1999), p. 328 et seq..
[168] Cf.: Wiskot, G. (2009), p. 246.
[169] Cf.: Wamser, J. (2005), p. 66.
[170] Cf.: Mehl-Lammens, P. (2006), p. 188.
[171] Cf.: Todd, P. R. / Javalgi, R. G. (2007), p. 173.
[172] Cf.: Wiskot, G. (2009), p. 256.
[173] Cf.: Ossola-Haring, C. / Ruh, W. (2008), p. 29.
[174] Cf.: Germany Trade and Invest (2010), p. 43.
[175] Cf.: Wiskot, G. (2009), p. 257.
[176] Cf.: Todd, P. R. / Javalgi, R. G. (2007), p. 173.

Moreover, impediments can result from the strict labour law which is diversely handled in different federal states.[177] A multitude of labour laws consisting of 50 centralized laws and more than 150 regulations of the different federal states exist whereupon these clauses are often inconsistent.[178]

Companies with more than one hundred employees need to obtain approvals for personnel reductions, factory displacements and closing whereupon these permissions are seldom granted. Therefore a plenty of Indian medium-sized enterprises start series of businesses with small companies instead of large concerns.[179] Another widely-used possibility to avoid approval obtaining is to develop so-called "Voluntary Retirement Schemes" or to pay compensation.[180] In addition, many companies recruit required employees with the help of temporary employment agencies to reduce the amount of permanent workers.[181] As a result, German small and medium-sized enterprises should be aware of the strict regulations applying for companies with more than 100 employees when entering the Indian market to avoid subsequent impediments.

Reforms of the labour law should be implemented to extend the employment rate especially in large companies as they are restricted by laws and impeded to realize economies of scale. By the enforcement of reforms the employment, productivity, real wages and the number of social benefit recipients would increase.[182]

Additional barriers can follow from the forbidden child labour. Therefore German companies should define concrete specifications and sanctions against Indian partners or suppliers in connection with child labour. Notwithstanding of the social and ethical aspects, child labour is criminal, official assignments are prohibited and the image is damaged.[183] Foreign investors should try to defend themselves from child labour by demanding certificates from Indian companies confirming that the goods are produced without the assignment of people younger than 14 years.[184]

---

177 Cf.: Wiskot, G. (2009), p. 259.
178 Cf.: Weidlich, T. et al. (2011), p. 92.
179 Cf.: Wiskot, G. (2009), p. 258.
180 Cf.: DE International (2011), p. 6.
181 Cf.: Ossola-Haring, C. / Ruh, W. (2008), p. 88.
182 Cf.: OECD (2007b), p. 5 et seq..
183 Cf.: Weidlich, T. et al. (2011), p. 76.
184 Cf.: Wiskot, G. (2009), p. 217.

5.2.4. Non-tariff barriers for German small and medium-sized companies

For the validation if the above mentioned non-tariff barriers also apply to small and medium-sized companies, questions regarding import regulations and cooperation with different institutions were asked.

The majority of the questionnaire respondents rated the collaboration with public administration and authorities as "bad" or "very bad". In contrast, the cooperation with financial institutions has a better performance according to the participants.[185] In this regard, the managing director of a consultancy company stated that administrative procedures take long and regulations are handled differently by diverse authorities. Therefore processes are confusing and can not be scheduled.[186] Furthermore, patience and well-functioning bank contacts are required for good cooperation with financial institutes. Otherwise, money transfers can take months.[187]

Within three interviews the respondents pointed out that particular attention needs to be paid to contracts as these are complicated and various details should be included.[188]

Additionally, the inquiries of the interviewees underlined that the high bureaucracy is the key non-tariff barriers in India as 50 per cent of the interviewees reported that their businesses are hindered by the high bureaucracy.[189]

The in the literature mentioned non-tariff barriers resulting from strict labour laws, the Indian license system, the forbidden child labour, comprehensive environmental protect laws, plagiarising of merchandise and counterfeited products as well as lack of privacy, security and liability were not relevant for the respondent companies. Nevertheless, these impediments should be taken into consideration by companies entering the Indian market.

185 Cf.: Appendix 2, p. XX; p. XXI.
186 Cf.: Appendix 3, Interview 1, p. XLIX.
187 Cf.: Appendix 3, Interview 7, p. LXX.
188 Cf.: Appendix 3, Interview 9, p. LXXIV; Interview 11, p. LXXXI; Interview 12, p. LXXXII.
189 Cf.: Appendix 3, Interview 1, p. XLIX; Interview 4, p. LXI; Interview 6, p. LXV; Interview 8, p. LXXII; Interview 9, p. LXXIII; Interview 14, p. LXXXVIII.

5.3. Market-related barriers

India's growth is especially impeded by the insufficient infrastructure which is reflected by shabby airports, overloaded harbours, perforated roads and permanent electrical power outages.[190]

In this study market-related barriers are determined as all non-governmental constraints resulting from conditions which are unswayable by an individual company as described in chapter two.

5.3.1. Impediments resulting from India's infrastructure in relation of transport, communication and estate

The qualitative state of highways, traffic jams and long waiting times at customs facilities permit an average speed of 30 to 40 km/h which frequently leads to delays. Even though, India offers one of the longest railway systems worldwide, the transportation of goods is tedious due to long loadings and unloadings as well as the average speed of about 25 km/h.[191] Therefore many companies shifted the transport to highways due to the deterioration of the railway system.[192] Moreover, Indian harbours are undeveloped and overloaded whereupon the unloading of a ship takes ten times longer than in other harbours. Additionally, modern container-ships cannot be dispatched due to their sizes. Some ships have to wait up to 30 days until they can be unloaded due to blockages of docks.[193] The quality of airports is also unsatisfying whereupon the air freight is the most qualitative means of transport, but also the most expensive.[194]

The inadequate transport infrastructure leads to higher warehouse capacities and charges whereupon just-in-time deliveries are seldom realizable[195] therefore customer proximity is important to deliver efficiently services. Frequently, delays of imports occur because of capacity constraints resulting from scarce human resources and infrastructural misconnection to the back country. Long customs handlings lead to additional storage costs and goods can be spoiled due to the

[190] Cf.: Müller, O. (2006), p. 27.
[191] Cf.: Waldkirch, K. (2006), p. 89 et seq..
[192] Cf.: Weidlich, T. et al. (2011), p. 17.
[193] Cf.: Pilny, K. (2006), p. 64.
[194] Cf.: Germany Trade and Invest (2010), p. 64.
[195] Cf.: Holtbrugge, D. / Friedmann, C. B. (2011), p. 277.

extreme climatic conditions. Therefore suitable packages and temperate storehouses are required for dispatching and stocking easily soiled and temperature sensitive products.[196] Higher storage costs can also result from strikes of suppliers and carriers as well as from long waiting times due to border crossings and custom facilities.[197]

In spite of the high economic growth, India is not able to subsidize these investments.[198] Moreover, many citizens appeal against the construction of dams and motorways in front of their houses as well as against the demolition of slums which lead to deferments of large-scale projects.[199] For solving one of the most essential barriers, investments of approximately USD 500 billion are required for the development of the infrastructure. Therefore privatisation and Public Private Partnerships (PPP) are supported by the government for example with the permission of 100 per cent foreign direct investment in infrastructural projects.[200]

India's telecommunication sector is comparatively well developed and India belongs to one of the country with the lowest charges worldwide whereupon five million telephone connections are added each month.[201] Nevertheless, India possesses a low distribution of modern technology and a low diffusion process. On average, the technologic equipment of India is low and is in accordance with other developing countries.[202]

Land prices as well as rents for offices and other commercial premises are rising due to the lasting economic growth. In the near of metropolis land for building is scarce and increasingly more expensive due to the high demand.[203]
Many Indians do not accept responsibility for collective domains such as for houses, flats, waste disposal or street cleaning thus the quality is adversely affected which is intensified by the monsoon and environmental pollution.[204]

---

[196] Cf.: Germany Trade and Invest (2010), p. 30 et seqq..
[197] Cf.: Dülfer, E. (1999), p. 407.
[198] Cf.: Pilny, K. (2006), p. 65.
[199] Cf.: Müller, O. (2006), p. 27.
[200] Cf.: Pilny, K. (2006), p. 65.
[201] Cf.: Wiskot, G. (2009), p. 207.
[202] Cf.: Wamser, J. (2005), p. 70.
[203] Cf.: Weidlich, T. et al. (2011), p. 101.
[204] Cf.: Wiskot, G. (2009), p. 117.

In general, the searching of suitable locations prove to be difficult especially for tenderfoots due to confusing offers thus renowned real estate agencies can be recommended. On the contrary, small, regional property dealer have a dubious reputation and caution is advisable. Moreover, German investors should check if the desired business activity is allowed at the respective location as rental objects are often offered for commercial use without permission. Subsequently, investors have to pay high penalties and the office needs to be closed in the course of governmental inspections.[205]

Especially, the manufacturing industry suffers from the insufficient infrastructure and production downtimes due to electrical power outages. According to the actual five-year plan, India needs about one trillion US Dollars for the development of the infrastructure whereupon domestic and foreign companies are called on to invest in this sector.[206]

5.3.2. Impediments resulting from water and electricity supply

Absent or scarce water and electrical power supply are one of the highest investment barriers for the economic growth in India[207] whereupon the demand for energy exceeds the demand by 16 per cent countrywide.[208] Besides deficient electric power stations, especially high conduction losses of about 50 per cent due to bad maintenances, out-dated conductions and electricity thefts resulting in increased shortages. Electrical power outages and current fluctuations daily occur in most of the regions which lead amongst other things to damages at electrical devises thus investors install emergency generators to secure sufficient electrical power supply.[209] Consequently, the energy deficit restrains the development of the Indian economic growth. Moreover high energy prices are influencing the industrial production and the dependencies on oil as well as its shortages cause India's economic slowdown.[210] The share on renewable energy will be increasingly more important, economic development schemes are supported by the government and 100 per cent foreign direct investments are permitted in the sector of renewable energy. Especially the know-how of German solar companies in regard to project

[205] Cf.: Germany Trade and Invest (2010), p. 108 et seqq..
[206] Cf.: Weidlich, T. et al. (2011), p. 8.
[207] Cf.: Waldkirch, K. (2006), p. 89.
[208] Cf.: Pilny, K. (2006), p. 64.
[209] Cf.: Wiskot, G. (2009), p. 35 et seqq..
[210] Cf.: Waldkirch, K. (2006), p. 23 et seqq..

planning, plant construction as well as in the training of technical skilled employees is high in demand.[211]

In India, the supply water is not drinkable and in many places the groundwater is contaminated with pesticides. The groundwater level is too low and more wells are needed, that is the reason why twelve metropolises obtain just 70 per cent of the daily water demand and the deficit is compensated with the help of expensive emergency supplies.[212]

5.3.3. Impediments concerning the Indian labour market

Despite the huge amount of degree holders, some industries are not able to find sufficient skilled human resources. This development is impeded by the high illiteracy and the existing deficits in the academic education.[213] The educational system cannot keep up with the population growth and balance the existing social and regional differences. Especially, state-owned schools possess low quality due to the lack of qualified teachers and few financial as well as material resources.[214] The government increased investments in education to improve the school system whereupon the respective federal states have the competencies for education and thus urgencies are differently seen.[215] In addition, theoretical knowledge is given priority in the Indian education system and practical experiences as well as soft skills are seldom pronounced. Therefore learning-on-the-job is a common practice whereupon this process can take years for complicated applications and frequently skilled workers are headhunted by other companies.

Graduates prefer employments in the remunerative IT sector whereupon other branches are often confronted with shortage of skilled labour.[216] Frequently, the amount of qualified employees does not satisfy the demand for experienced and skilled labours thus their salaries are rising and personnel shortages will deteriorate the future.[217] Salary increases continuously account for 10 or 15 per cent per year,

---

[211] Cf.: Wildemann, H. / Engelmeier, T. (2011), p. 1.
[212] Cf.: Wiskot, G. (2009), p. 189.
[213] Cf.: Weidlich, T. et al. (2011), p. 91.
[214] Cf.: Handelskammer Hamburg (2010), s.p..
[215] Cf.: Zotz, V. (2006), p. 92.
[216] Cf.: Germany Trade and Invest (2010), p. 78.
[217] Cf.: Rodewald, A. (2007), p. 62 et seqq..

reaching partially the level of industrialized countries. Nevertheless, in many industries the wage level remains lower than in other Asian countries.[218]
In general, the level of salaries differs depending on the respective industry, region and employees' qualifications. Salaries often include tax-deductible benefits such as flats, gratuities, provision of cars and chauffeurs, health care, tuition for children as well as additional individual benefits.[219]

Moreover, German companies should account for a high labour turnover due to higher earnings in competing companies resulting in additional cost for job trainings and issues for start-ups.[220] Labour turnovers can be reduced by agreements in relation to long periods of notice or to bonds.[221] Human resource bindings can be eased by further trainings whereupon the repayment of the costs should be graded in terms of resignation depending on the employee's seniority.[222]

To sum up, the recruitment of well-trained and loyal employees is difficult due to the multitude of applications and the lack of practical experiences of graduates resulting in an initially high fault rate and a long training period.[223]

5.3.4. Impediments resulting from climatic and environmental conditions

The imponderability of the monsoon often destroys harvests, hinders the industrial production and corporate-policy decisions.[224] Transports are also restrained by the monsoon due to flowed roads. In addition, the insufficient infrastructure demands for the closeness of warehouses to customers to avoid long delivery times, delays and damages. Especially, sensitive products can be damaged due to extreme changing weather conditions, high temperatures and humidity. However, the supply of modern warehouses protecting goods against environmental influences does not meet the demand resulting in high costs.[225]
In spite of the comprehensive environment protect laws their implementation is still malfunctioned due to the lack of competencies, local private interests and the distinctive corruption. The awareness of the Indian population in relation to envi-

[218] Cf.: Weidlich, T. et al. (2011), p. 91 et seq..
[219] Cf.: DE International (2011), p. 5.
[220] Cf.: Zotz, V. (2006), p. 98.
[221] Cf.: Wiskot, G. (2009), p. 258.
[222] Cf.: Waldkirch, K. (2006), p. 117.
[223] Cf.: Ossola-Haring, C. / Ruh, W. (2008), p. 71.
[224] Cf.: Dülfer, E. (1999), p. 239.
[225] Cf.: Germany Trade and Invest (2010), p. 62.

ronmental protection is marginal whereas the government tries to increase this consciousness as environmental awareness is a school subject in primary schools. In this conjunction, the main issues are air pollution in big cities, unavailability of potable water, consumption of natural resources and the deforestation of rainforests. In metropolitan areas such as Mumbai and Delhi taxis and busses were equipped with gas engines which led to an ameliorated air quality. The cleanness of water in rivers and lakes as well as the related drinking water quality are further central issues of the Indian environment. Sewage works are still uncirculated, sewage water pollutes districts, about 80 per cent of the town rubbish is trashed in rivers and 55 per cent of the urban apartment houses are not connected to the sewerage system.[226]

Nevertheless, the insignificance of the manufacturing industry leads to less environmental pollution compared to China whereby air pollution and destructive exploitation are increasing. This development is intensified by undeveloped coal-fired power stations causing immense emissions to reduce the energy deficit.[227]

5.3.5. Impediments resulting from corruption

Despite India is the largest democracy worldwide, corruption is widespread in policy and executive[228] as many politicians strive for their maintenance of power.[229] According to the corruption perception index 2011, India is a corruptive country by reaching place 96 of 182 countries.[230] Generally, Indian companies settle speed money because the payment for approvals is cheaper than proceedings against authorities.[231] Projects that are announced by state-owned enterprises or governmental departments are often influenced by corruption. The cheapest party tendering receives the acceptance of the tender and has to pay a bribe to the authority. Consequently, the quality suffers from productions at low prices whereupon this handling can be especially observed in the road construction.[232]
The daily business is affected by corruption as officers claim donations for the processing of applications.

---

[226] Cf.: Wiskot, G. (2009), p. 193 et seq..
[227] Cf.: Pilny, K. (2006), p. 67.
[228] Cf.: Chopin, C. (2009), p. 8.
[229] Cf.: Wamser, J. (2005), p. 69.
[230] Cf.: Transparency International Deutschland e.V. (2011), s.p..
[231] Cf.: Rodewald, A. (2007), p. 105.
[232] Cf.: Mehl-Lammens, P. (2006), p. 182.

Foreign investors should not pay these donations and should retain so-called clearance agents to clarify governmental affairs as they are familiar with bribes and know the responsible decision-makers.[233] Corruption is a punishable crime for all involved parties and companies can be blacklisted which lead to a prohibition for further economical activities.[234] Furthermore, corruption is prosecuted in Germany, even though the donation was paid in India.[235]

The extension of corruption should be significantly minimized as India's reliability is at risk for foreign investors and domestic economic activities are restrained.[236]

5.3.6. India's worldwide reputation and Germany's image in India

India's international reputation remains bad, particularly Germans perceive India as a developing country and not as a business location with increasing potential for the future. The socio-political general conditions are still problematic due to conflicts between diverse ethnic groups resulting in terrorist assaults, increasing religious influences on politics and growing socio-economic disparities.[237] Social conflicts often result from religious contexts such as between Hindus and Muslims therefore religious conditions have to be considered in relation to location decisions, recruitments and buildings of teams to avoid disputes.[238] On the other hand businesses are transacted between all religions.[239] According to an international comparative study India belongs to one of the 25th most political risky countries worldwide.[240]

Products made in Germany are ranking high in India due to their quality, reliability and technical longevity. In addition, Indians appreciate the German punctuality and thoroughness.[241] On the other hand, Germans are considered to be reserved, harsh, unfriendly and always in a hurry.[242]

---

233 Cf.: Wiskot, G. (2009), p. 184.
234 Cf.: Zotz, V. (2006), p. 93.
235 Cf.: Germany Trade and Invest (2010), p. 24.
236 Cf.: Pilny, K. (2006), p. 55.
237 Cf.: Wamser, J. (2005), p. 77.
238 Cf.: Zotz, V. (2006), p. 75.
239 Cf.: Mehl-Lammens, P. (2006), p. 50.
240 Cf.: Wamser, J. (2005), p. 77.
241 Cf.: Rodewald, A. (2007), p. 24 et seqq..
242 Cf.: Ossola-Haring, C. / Ruh, W. (2008), p. 30.

5.3.7. Market-related barriers for German small and medium-sized companies

For analysing if the mentioned market-related barriers apply to German small and medium-sized companies, the participating companies where asked to specify which impediments affect their businesses.

In general, the given responds vary dependent on the respective location. This study does not analyse different locations in India as insufficient responds were provided by the consulted companies. Therefore the given information cannot be generalized and no recommendations about the choice of locations can be made. For reducing impediments resulting from the respective location, environmental analysis should be made by German investors.

Divers questions were asked about the Indian transport infrastructure with the help of the questionnaire whereupon in each case the availability and the quality were assessed by the participants. In general, the availability of the Indian infrastructure performed better than its quality.
The availability of itineraries, especially in regard of international transportation was rated as "good" by the majority of the respondents.[243] On the contrary, the quality of the local public and the national transportation was evaluated as "bad" or "very bad" by more than 70 per cent of the consulted companies. However, the quality of international transportation was appraised as "good" by 67 per cent of the participants.[244] In conjunction with the transport infrastructure the consulted companies were asked to evaluate the cost of transport. Although the quality of the local public as well as national transportation were generally assessed as "bad",[245] 62 per cent of the respondents were satisfied with the cost of transport.[246]
According to the literature, the transport infrastructure is considered to be one of the major barriers for foreign investors whereas the consulted small and medium-sized companies did not attach importance to this impediment as it was not mentioned by one of the interviewees.

---

243 Cf.: Appendix 2, p. XXV; p. XXVI.
244 Cf.: Appendix 2, p. XXXI.
245 Cf.: Appendix 2, p. XXX; p. XXXI.
246 Cf.: Appendix 2, p. XXXVIII.

In general, the availability of communication systems is assessed better than its quality by the participants. However, the availability and the quality of phone and fax as well as internet and email were evaluated as "high" or "very high" by the majority of the questionnaire respondents.[247] In comparison, the availability of the postal system was rated as "high" by 44 per cent and as "low" by 40 per cent and its quality as "good" by 30 per cent and as "bad" by 44 per cent of the consulted companies.[248] This is underlined by a statement given by the managing director of a consultancy company stating that the postal delivery can take long, is unreliable and the payment of bribe is often required as corruption is widespread.[249]
Building on that, the communication systems should be especially improved in terms of its postal system.

The Indian property market was categorized as "bad" by the majority of the questionnaire respondents whereupon the availability was better evaluated than its quality. Especially, the quality of buildings and office spaces was rated as "bad" or "very bad" by more than 70 per cent of the participants.[250] Furthermore, the consulted companies were asked about their satisfaction with rents and site costs whereupon 64 per cent were "dissatisfied" or "very dissatisfied".[251] This evaluation is underlined by the fact that three interviewees explicitly named the quality of buildings and rooms as an issue relating to the Indian infrastructure.[252] One employee belonging to the middle management of a food industry company suggested the rent or purchase of new rooms or buildings as the costs for maintenance and repair are consistent with the costs and efforts of new estates.[253]

The availability as well as the quality of the Indian electricity supply was rated as "bad" or "very bad" by the vast majority of the respondents.[254] According to three interviewees, electrical power outages often occur in India whereupon the usage of generators is required which lead to additional costs.[255]

---

[247] Cf.: Appendix 2, p. XXVII; XXVIII; p. XXXIII.
[248] Cf.: Appendix 2, p. XXVIII; p. XXXIV.
[249] Cf.: Appendix 3, Interview 1, p. L.
[250] Cf.: Appendix 2, p. XXIX, p. XXXV.
[251] Cf.: Appendix 2, p. XXXVII.
[252] Cf.: Appendix 3, Interview 1, p. L; Interview 6, p. LXVI; Interview 12, p. LXXXIII.
[253] Cf.: Appendix 3, Interview 6, p. LXVI.
[254] Cf.: Appendix 2, p. XXVI; p. XXVII; p. XXXII.
[255] Cf.: Appendix 3, Interview 1, p. XLIX; Interview 6, p. LXVI; Interview 14, p. LXXXVIII.

Although the availability of the water supply is considered to be better than the electricity supply, its quality is regarded as "bad" or "very bad" by 77 per cent of the participants.[256] The managing director of a consultancy company stated that the water is dirty and undrinkable. Moreover, less than 10 per cent of the Indian population have access to toilets and sewage systems are seldom which lead to bad environmental conditions and diseases.[257]

In addition, the participating companies were interrogated about the labour market to identify if impediments result for small and medium-sized companies. In this relation, the availability of manpower was evaluated as "good" or "very good" by 80 per cent of the questionnaire respondents.[258] The consulted companies were also satisfied with labour and wage costs as it was assessed as "good" or "very good" by 74 per cent of the participants.[259] In connection with the labour market the level of training and qualifications performed worst as it was rated as "good" or "very good" by 52 per cent of the respondents.[260] Furthermore, the managing director of a lawyer's office adds that high labour turnovers and salary increases in clusters such as Delhi, Poona, Chennai, Hyderabad, Kolkata and Bangalore affect the labour market. On the other hand, the employees possess the best level of training and education in these clusters.[261] Moreover, one employee of the chamber of commerce and industry reported that the number of degree holders and unskilled workers are high whereas the amount of skilled engineering workers is insufficient. Additionally, she stated that companies should compare different universities to identify their qualities and thereby the qualifications of the degree holders.[262] In addition, the managing director of a consultancy company obtained information by numerous companies that the educational level is bad in India. Highly skilled employees are trained abroad and their labour costs are as high as in Germany. In India trained employees often possess theoretical knowledge thus further trainings are necessary to acquire practical abilities for the deployment in companies. In addition, she pointed out that the educational material of universities is frequently out-of-date.[263] One employee belonging to the middle management of a food

---

[256] Cf.: Appendix 2, p. XXXII.
[257] Cf.: Appendix 3, Interview 1, p. XLIX.
[258] Cf.: Appendix 2, p. XIV.
[259] Cf.: Appendix 2, p. XV; p. XXXVI.
[260] Cf.: Appendix 2, p. XIV.
[261] Cf.: Appendix 3, Interview 12, p. LXXXII.
[262] Cf.: Appendix 3, Interview 14, p. LXXXVIII.
[263] Cf.: Appendix 3, Interview 5, p. LXII.

industry company warns investors of the misjudgement of labour and wage costs as in India more employees than in Germany are needed due to the bad education which result in higher costs.[264]

In relation to the standard of life five questions were asked to the companies whereupon the availability of flats and houses as well as the security in India performed better than health care, climate and environment.

The availability of houses and flats was rated as "good" by 42 per cent and as "bad" by 34 per cent of the questionnaire participants.[265] The managing director of a lawyer's office reported that the availability of flats and houses is insufficient, especially at reasonable prices. According to her, flats and houses are expensive in quarters inhabited by Europeans as international schools, gardeners and chauffeurs met the standard.[266] Two interviewees pointed out that rents and land prices are high, but their quality is low, especially in areas with a high population density.[267]

In relation to health care, security and climatic conditions no common statement can be made which is caused by India's diversity. The Indian health care is evaluated as "bad" by 47 per cent whereas it is appraised as "good" by 43 per cent of the participating companies.[268] More than the half of the respondents assessed the security in India as "good" in comparison to 32 per cent of the companies considering the security as "bad".[269] 52 per cent of the participants rated the climatic conditions as "bad" and 38 per cent as "good".[270] This evaluation can be constituted by the heat and the monsoon whereupon the enormous heat is named as one issue by four interviewees.[271]

In connection with the subject "standard of life" the worst responds were given to the question concerning the environmental conditions as it is considered to be "very bad" by 54 per cent and to be "bad" by 33 per cent of the participating companies.[272] According to one employee belonging to the middle management of a constructions and machine building industry the reason for the India's poor envi-

[264] Cf.: Appendix 3, Interview 6, p. LXVIII.
[265] Cf.: Appendix 2, p. XL.
[266] Cf.: Appendix 3, Interview 12, p. LXXXIV.
[267] Cf.: Appendix 3, Interview 1, p. L; Interview 6, p. LXVI.
[268] Cf.: Appendix 2, p. XL.
[269] Cf.: Appendix 2, p. XLI.
[270] Cf.: Appendix 2, p. XLI.
[271] Cf.: Appendix 3, Interview 1, p. L; Interview 4, p. LX; Interview 11, p. LXXX; Interview 12, p. LXXXIV.
[272] Cf.: Appendix 2, p. XLII.

ronmental quality are constituted by its noise, dirt and enormous heat. Moreover, he stated that the environment is disregarded by many manufacturing industries especially in connection with the refuse destruction and sewage in rivers.[273]

According to the literature, foreign investors are not hindered by business market conditions therefore this subject was not considered so far. However, questions concerning the business market were asked to small and medium-sized companies for the verification if impediments arise for them.

In this connection, 95 per cent of the questionnaire respondents assessed the economic climate as "good" or "very good".[274] This positive result is affirmed by the evaluation of the domestic market demand as it is rated as "high" or "very high" by about 80 per cent of the consulted companies.[275] Therefore German investors should be concentrated on domestic customers instead of low-cost production for exports at reasonably priced products. This recommendation is also underlined by the quantity of Indian customers as 39 per cent of the participating companies rated them as "high" and 33 per cent as "very high".[276]

To sum up, neither big nor small and medium-sized companies are negatively influenced by the Indian business market thus German investors should seize the chance for investing in India as long as the economic climate is satisfying.

Moreover, the participating companies assessed the prevalence of corruption in India as high. In this connection, respondents named public administration and authorities as well as politics as the sectors with the highest distribution of bribery. Nevertheless, 38 per cent of the respondents admit that they have been asked to pay a bribe before.[277] However, nine of 14 interviewees named corruption as an important impediment.[278] In the context of the tender subject "corruption" one employee belonging to the middle management of an automotive supplier stated that the participation in the payment of bribe is forbidden by German corporate compliances and German companies can lose their good reputation and have to reckon with legal consequences. In addition, he admitted that the payment of 100

[273] Cf.: Appendix 3, Interview 4, p. LX.
[274] Cf.: Appendix 2, p. XIX.
[275] Cf.: Appendix 2, p. XVI.
[276] Cf.: Appendix 2, p. XVII.
[277] Cf.: Appendix 2, p. XXII; p. XXIII.
[278] Cf.: Appendix 3, Interview 1, p. L; Interview 2, p. LIII; Interview 3, p. LVII; Interview 4, p. LX; Interview 5, p. LXIII; Interview 7, p. LXX; Interview 8, p. LXXII; Interview 10, p. LXXVII; Interview 14, p. LXXXVIII.

rupees is cheaper than regularly flying to India to clarify issues on-site. According to his statement, Indian as well as South African and Asian companies are better prepared with the subject "corruption". These companies are able to gain competitive advantages by benefiting from quicker processes of approving and thus reacting faster on changes of the market. Moreover, he noted that local experts are necessary as they are familiar with the subject corruption and know whom to pay which amount of bribe.[279]

The cooperation with policy-makers was rated as rated as "bad" or "very bad" by the majority of the questionnaire respondents.[280] One reason for this evaluation is the high bureaucracy and the corruptibility according to two interviewees.[281] In addition, the managing director of a consultancy companies reported that conflicts between the both most influential parties lead to numerous changes of the Indian tax system and import regulations.[282] Despite the bad assessment of the cooperation with policy-makers, the Indian political stability was considered to be "good" by 54 per cent of the consulted companies.[283]

Concluding, the most important market-related barriers for small and medium-sized companies are the insufficient electricity and water supply, the environmental conditions, the high corruption and the cooperation with policy-makers as well as the property market.

5.4. Company-related barriers

Differences between the German and the Indian business culture are often underestimated by German investors as they assume that cultural diversities do not influence business activities. Therefore needless risks are often taken and a multitude of business opportunities cannot be availed due to the complexity of India's cultural basic conditions as well as the cultural distances between India and Germany.[284]

[279] Cf.: Appendix 3, Interview 3, p. LVII.
[280] Cf.: Appendix 2, p. XXI.
[281] Cf.: Appendix 3, Interview 4, p. LX; Interview 6, p. LXV.
[282] Cf.: Appendix 3, Interview 1, p. LI.
[283] Cf.: Appendix 2, p. XXII.
[284] Cf.: Wamser, J. (2005), p. 95.

In this study company-related barriers are determined as all non-governmental impediments which are influenceable by an individual company or which affect the daily business of a single company.

5.4.1. Impediments concerning the personnel recruitment and human resource management

Initially, the recruitment of the middle and upper hierarchical level are recommended whereupon headhunting agencies are advisable as they have sufficient experience to evaluate information provided in curricula vitae and during job interviews. Executive employees can be assigned for the personnel engagement of inferior positions.[285] In this regard, executive position should be filled with seniors as employees show more respect to older people.[286] Moreover, management positions can be filled by repatriates as they are trained in westernized countries and thus are familiar with both cultures.
The bottom line is that an Indian local recruited management is more suitable due to its market knowledge as well as its established business relationships.[287]

As religion and caste is a complex subject, German companies should consult domestic human resource experts in regard of the recruitment and buildings of teams to avoid conflicts within teams. If someone of a lower caste (Dalit) is nominated as team leader, employees of upper castes (Brahmin) can be annoyed which can lead to conflicts and disruptions.[288] Additionally, German manager should respect religious minorities and cultures as well as their customs and traditions.[289]

One important aspect of the Hinduism and the caste system is the acquittal of the respective function or task thus the working morale is high whereby additional obligations have to be fixed in targeted appraisal interviews.[290] Based on this understanding, so-called "boys" are employed in Indian companies carrying out menial jobs such as opening doors, bringing drinks or carrying records. These activities would not be performed by Indian supervisors as they would lose their

[285] Cf.: Germany Trade and Invest (2010), p. 80 et seq..
[286] Cf.: Ossola-Haring, C. / Ruh, W. (2008), p. 71.
[287] Cf.: Germany Trade and Invest (2010), p. 80.
[288] Cf.: Mehl-Lammens, P. (2006), p. 52.
[289] Cf.: Waldkirch, K. (2006), p. 112.
[290] Cf.: Zotz, V. (2006), p. 75.

reputation.[291] German companies should pay attention to this high distribution of tasks to avoid conflicts between labour forces. Consequently, more workers are employed in Indian companies resulting in additional costs.

In Germany the individualism is widespread, however equity is presupposed for the social interaction. On the other hand, in India collective awareness in relation to caste and family is characteristic and individualism is less pronounced. In addition, inequality and hierarchy are accepted by Indians due to the Hinduism which lead to rigid rankings, absent equity, unchangeable constraints and unequal distribution of power and authority.[292] Therefore the acquittal of the respective function also influences the Indian society which is a high power-distance culture as employees favour authoritative and hierarchical structures.[293]

Indians expect managers to lead employees in all concerns which are a mark of respect as managers are considered to be omniscient.[294] Clear job descriptions and detailed orders are necessary to create worker enthusiasm and motivation. On the other hand, the democratic management style of German managers is considered as weakness or incompetence.[295] Therefore managers should have good soft skills such as leadership skills if they are leading a company in India as individual contacts are more important than expert knowledge. Indian employees are motivated by continuously recognition, respect and appreciation.[296]

In addition, managers are taken seriously if they have a family-oriented background.[297] In this context, German managers should consider that families are of great value in India. Frequently, family members are recommended by Indians in case of recruitments and contract awards thus nepotism is a common practice in India. In this connection, public holidays should be individually listed in each company as they are diverse in different federal states and should be observed, as Indians are sensitive if these days are neglected due to their family ties.[298]

---

[291] Cf.: Wiskot, G. (2009), p. 236 et seqq..
[292] Cf.: Wamser, J. (2005), p. 97.
[293] Cf.: Davis, H. J. D. et al. (2006), p. 32.
[294] Cf.: Mitterer, K. et al. (2006), p. 24.
[295] Cf.: Davis, H. J. D. et al. (2006), p. 32.
[296] Cf.: Mehl-Lammens, P. (2006), p. 93 et seqq.
[297] Cf.: Zotz, V. (2006), p. 55.
[298] Cf.: Wiskot, G. (2009), p. 237 et seqq..

Frequently, the quality of work does not meet the expectation of German managers whereupon simultaneous trainings, quality specifications and monitoring can lead to the designated quality.

Additionally, the planning and organisation are considered to be chaotic from a western point of view thus the German mother company should establish precise basic conditions for the subsidiary. Deadlines and performance goals should be set out in writing whereupon the work process should be regularly overhauled and buffers should be scheduled. In this connection, the management by objective or Balanced Scorecards have proved in many companies managed by Germans whereupon bonuses are earned by employees if targets are achieved.[299]

5.4.2. Impediments resulting from the collaboration with other companies and from the quality of customers

The Indian culture is marked by a characteristic relationship orientation thus personal mutual trust is the basis for business contacts. According to that multiple meetings should be scheduled before contracts can be signed.[300] Long-term businesses with a win-win-situation for both business partners are aspired by a plenty of Indian tradesmen.[301]

This is also reflected by the distinctive networking whereupon German companies can benefit from Indians in relation to their networks with others Indians.[302]

The cooperation with a domestic company in the form of a joint venture or with the help of a business partner can reduce market entry barriers. Proponents argue that joint ventures benefit from greater financial resources, higher risk absorption, rapid access to knowledge and know-how, increased specialization and thus from enhanced efficiency.[303] On the other hand, cooperation can result in intercultural conflicts[304] and Indian partners can pursue different strategies thus partners should be handpicked.[305] In general, the cooperation with an Indian company in the form of a joint venture has been eased since 1st April 2011. The "Press Note No. 1 (2005)" was abolished whereupon existing investments in the context of joint ventures or

[299] Cf.: Mehl-Lammens, P. (2006), p. 77 et seq..
[300] Cf.: Mitterer, K. et al. (2006), p. 23.
[301] Cf.: Ossola-Haring, C. / Ruh, W. (2008), p. 40.
[302] Cf.: Mehl-Lammens, P. (2006), p. 28 et seq..
[303] Cf.: McAuley, A. (2001), p. 128.
[304] Cf.: Eschlbeck, D. (2006), p. 589.
[305] Cf.: Holtbrugge, D. / Friedmann, C. B. (2011), p. 276.

technical cooperation no longer need a permission of the state for consequential investments in the same economic sector.[306]

In India, supplies are often confronted with quality defects as just few suppliers observe international standards whereupon 80 per cent of the turnover in the branch is generated by small, family-run companies with out-of-date vehicles causing high accident rates and damages at the transported goods.[307] Therefore certifications and qualifications as well as technical support and further trainings for employees are necessary for granting high quality.[308] In addition, the quality of work of Indian business partners can be increased by the agreement of an intended date of notice as Indians often prefer long-term relationships.[309]

In conjunction with the cooperation with other companies but also with own employees, German managers should consider that Indians have a different concept of time which is also known as the Indian Standard Time (IST). As the term "time" is an everlasting cycle according to the Indian comprehension, exact points in time are not relevant. Descriptively, for the terms "yesterday" and "tomorrow" the same word "Kal" is used in Hindi. Nevertheless, punctuality is expected at commercial meetings, especially from German partners as Germans are considered to be punctual.[310] On the other side, date of delivery are often not failed to meet the deadline.[311]

The liquidity and creditworthiness of customers and suppliers should be screened whereupon data of the Indian Registrar of Companies are often out-of-date and electronically not available thus misinterpretations of potential partners are possible. This information can be obtained with the help of the Indo-German Chamber of Commerce. Generally, companies should only deliver if goods are paid on receipt or paid before as supplier' credits or acceptance bills are not advisable due to the extrajudicial unenforceability of outstanding debts.[312]

---

306 Cf.: Weidlich, T. et al. (2011), p. 20.
307 Cf.: Germany Trade and Invest (2010), p. 68.
308 Cf.: Holtbrugge, D. / Friedmann, C. B. (2011), p. 276.
309 Cf.: Mehl-Lammens, P. (2006), p. 188.
310 Cf.: Wiskot, G. (2009), p. 51 et seq..
311 Cf.: Dülfer, E. (1999), p. 407.
312 Cf.: Ossola-Haring, C. / Ruh, W. (2008), p. 37.

In general, the payment behaviour is often marked by delays thus businesses are eased by cash discount agreements, short-term projects or suspension of deliveries.[313] Frequently, the willingness to pay of Indian business partners is low and the effort to receive the agreed invoice amount is high whereupon persistency and regular reminders are necessary. According to the collection-indicator of Creditreform, India is ranking on the penultimate place of 30 leading national economics.[314]

5.4.3. Impediments concerning the marketing mix

German investors should regard India as heterogeneous market sectors due to its huge diversity which result in different customer requirements and demands. Therefore the location decision process should be conscientiously taken and target customers should be analyzed in regard of their preferences.[315]

Despite the continuously growing acceptance of western goods, overall the Indian consumers' behaviour remains relatively conservative.[316] A bulk of the population is afraid of a foreign infiltration as many Indians are deep-rooted with their traditions and culture.[317] Merely, a minority of the young urban middle class changed their traditional value system and are open-minded in regard to westernized standards. In general, Indians are loyal to private social values such as the arranged marriage and religious rituals. On the other hand, westernized cloths are dressed by Indians in the business world. Therefore the understanding of the nuances of the Indian culture is necessary to deal successfully with the Indian cultural complexity.[318]

In relation of the product developments, marketing and distribution channels the Indian diversity should be considered which is influenced by demographic, social and cultural aspects as well as by specific regional traditions, religion, climate and issues resulting of insufficient power supplies.[319]

In the context of the product policy, specific characteristics of the Indian market needs to be regarded such as shapes, colours, technical specifications and the

[313] Cf.: Wiskot, G. (2009), p. 246.
[314] Cf.: Germany Trade and Invest (2010), p. 40 et seq..
[315] Cf.: Waldkirch, K. (2006), p. 92.
[316] Cf.: Ossola-Haring, C. / Ruh, W. (2008), p. 35 et seqq..
[317] Cf.: Wamser, J. (2005), p. 75.
[318] Cf.: Wamser, J. (2005), p. 100.
[319] Cf.: Zotz, V. (2006), p. 122 et seqq..

usage of religious symbols. Therefore production adaptations are necessary, for example soil-resisting keyboards, small-sized packages for groceries and consumption goods of low value as well as electric devices with high-power batteries and high tolerances against voltage fluctuation.[320] The ingredients of groceries should be declared on packages in the respective local language as many Indians attend their food due to religious practices.[321] In addition, Indians of all income levels prefer luxury goods even though they are not able to afford them. Therefore luxury goods are produced at reasonable prices in downsized packages for the underclass.[322]

The Indian market is also characterized by high price elasticity, especially in regard of consumers with low incomes. Besides to a coordinated price policy, a suitable price communication is required to guarantee a product is noticed to be economically priced. This can be reached by sales approaches in the respective local language as well as by quantity discounts and loyalty programs.[323] Moreover, service is an efficient sales argument, especially for quality products that are sold at very high prices whereupon after sales services are expected by the customers.[324]

Additionally, convenience goods are bought in small stalls offering free of charge delivery services. This circumstance is often neglected by foreign companies whereby the volume of the retail industry is estimated to be about USD 330 billion thus good investment opportunities are offered. Once foreign investments are completely permitted in the retail industry, German small and medium-sized companies should take this opportunity to invest. Nowadays the amount of online shopping is rising due to costs savings, convenience and increased efficiency thus German small and medium-sized companies should take this possibility to sell their products via internet.[325]

Furthermore, communication channels are affected by the hierarchical organisation due to the circulation of information from the manager to the following hierarchy level and so on. Consequently, long communication channels can result in misun-

[320] Cf.: Holtbrugge, D. / Friedmann, C. B. (2011), p. 277.
[321] Cf.: Kirch, S. (2003), p. 23.
[322] Cf.: Ossola-Haring, C. / Ruh, W. (2008), p. 34.
[323] Cf.: Holtbrugge, D. / Friedmann, C. B. (2011), p. 277.
[324] Cf.: Germany Trade and Invest (2010), p. 21.
[325] Cf.: Ossola-Haring, C. / Ruh, W. (2008), p. 35 et seqq..

derstandings due to the relay of modified information. On the other hand, supervisors have to ask for information as they are not automatically informed by subordinates about the progress of a project.[326] Especially, negative information is repressed by employees.[327] Therefore quality or cost problems are hard to solve as employees often avoid informing supervisors about mistakes or delays.

Additionally, German supervisors should consider that in India an indirect communication style is used thus indirect feedbacks are common practice. Moreover, negations should be avoided and negative responds should be evasively given as Indians understand refusals as a personal defamation.[328] As Indians do not negatively reply to questions and do not admit that they do not understand or are not able to perform a task, supervisors should try to ask open or comprehension questions or should ask the employees to repeat the content of a task to minimize misunderstandings.[329]
For improving the communication within an international company, written communication procedures should be installed to increase the comprehension and to improve the flow of information.[330]

23 official languages can be seen as a further barrier whereupon English one of the official languages and is spoken by the educated business class.[331] Another issue in regard of communication is related to the silent language as facial expression, bearing and motions can be misinterpreted such as the Indian agreeing head cockling which is comparable with the negative European head shaking.[332]

5.4.4. Company-related barriers for German small and medium-sized companies

For the validation if the in the literature mentioned company-related barriers also apply to small and medium-sized companies, questions concerning company-related market barriers were asked.

---

[326] Cf.: Mitterer, K. et al. (2006), p. 40.
[327] Cf.: Waldkirch, K. (2006), p. 116.
[328] Cf.: Mehl-Lammens, P. (2006), p. 92 et seqq..
[329] Cf.: Wiskot, G. (2009), p. 239.
[330] Cf.: McAuley, A. (2001), p. 61 et seqq..
[331] Cf.: Kirch, S. (2003), p. 5.
[332] Cf.: Dülfer, E. (1999), p. 264.

In relation with the human resource management, the work ethic of the Indian employees was rated as "bad" or "very bad" by 65 per cent of the questionnaire respondents.[333] One employee belonging to the middle management of a food industry company stated that the management effort in India is higher as jobs and responsibilities can be more often delegated in Germany.[334] According to one employee belonging to the middle management of a constructions and machine building industry, Indian employees are hard to motivate due to the caste system and the acquittal of the respective function.[335]

Moreover, the consulted companies were asked with the help of the questionnaire which market entry barriers affect India's social framework. In this connection, issues concerning the Indian caste system were most frequently named, followed by the importance of the family. Impediments resulting from religion were mentioned by 10 per cent of the respondents[336] thus religion is not one of the most important barriers for German small and medium-sized companies.

In conjunction with the Indian caste system, one employee belonging to the middle management of a constructions and machine building industry stated that the membership to castes should be considered in regard of filling of executive positions as some Indian employees of the upper castes do not want to be led by workers from lower castes.[337] One interviewee reported that the job search and the matriculation at reputable universities are easier for sons of upper castes thus the caste system stuck in Indian's heads.[338] On the other hand, two consultancy companies mentioned that nowadays the caste system does not influence the business life.[339]

In relation to the importance of family, one employee belonging to the middle management of a food industry company affirmed that families can affect the business life as they often take the decision about family members' employments. Additionally, religious public holidays are also important and should be considered as families are used to spend these days together. Otherwise, employees can be annoyed and keep off the workplace.[340]

---

333 Cf.: Appendix 2, p. XV.
334 Cf.: Appendix 3, Interview 6, p. LXVI.
335 Cf.: Appendix 3, Interview 4, p. LXI.
336 Cf.: Appendix 2, p. XLVII.
337 Cf.: Appendix 3, Interview 5, p. LXIV.
338 Cf.: Appendix 3, Interview 3, p. LIX.
339 Cf.: Appendix 3, Interview 2, p. LV; Interview 9, p. LXXIV.
340 Cf.: Appendix 3, Interview 6, p. LXVIII.

According to the questionnaires, the most important intercultural challenges for the participating small and medium-sized in regard of their market entry were related to the know how of the Indian mentality, different perception of time and language barriers.[341] The managing director of a constructions and machine building company mentioned that the put pressure on Indians by Germans in regard of businesses is not understand by Indians as they have a different perception of time and the term "time" is stretched.[342] On the contrary, the managing director of a software company stated that the westernized perception of time is almost adapted by Indians in the business life resulting in fewer conflicts between Europeans and Indians.[343]

Furthermore, the cooperation with other companies was assessed as "good" by 64 per cent of the questionnaire respondents.[344] On the contrary, the collaboration with service providers performed worst as it was evaluated as "bad" by 40 per cent whereupon it was rated as "good" by at least 44 per cent.[345] The managing director of a lawyer's office admitted that quality controls of suppliers are harder to implement for small and medium-sized companies.[346]
Even though the multitude of the responding small and medium-sized companies were satisfied with the domestic market demand and the quantity of customers, 62 per cent of participants rated the customer's quality as "bad" or "very bad".[347] However, the consulted small and medium-sized companies did not attach importance to this impediment as it was not mentioned by one of the interviewees.

Additionally, the questionnaire respondents were asked about their evaluation of their general operating costs, revenues and profits and India's market potential. In this connection, the multitude of the participating small and medium-sized companies was satisfied with the general operating costs.[348] On the contrary, 40 per cent of the questionnaire respondents rated their revenues and profits as "good" or "very good".[349] This evaluation can be explained with the argument of two interviewees

---

[341] Cf.: Appendix 2, p. XLVII.
[342] Cf.: Appendix 3, Interview 7, p. LXX.
[343] Cf.: Appendix 3, Interview 9, p. LXXIV.
[344] Cf.: Appendix 2, p. XIX.
[345] Cf.: Appendix 2, p. XX.
[346] Cf.: Appendix 3, Interview 12, p. LXXXII.
[347] Cf.: Appendix 2, p. XVII.
[348] Cf.: Appendix 2, p. XXXVI.
[349] Cf.: Appendix 2, p. XVIII.

stating that the price sensitivity is high in India thus profit margins are low.[350] Nevertheless, the market potential is evaluated as "good" or "very good" by 92 per cent of the replying companies.[351]

To sum up, the most important company-related barriers for small and medium-sized companies are resulting from the work ethic, caste system, importance of family, different perception of time, collaboration with service providers and high price elasticity.

5.5. Recommendations, success factors and key challenges for German small and medium-sized companies in India

This chapter is dedicated to recommendations for effectually entering the Indian market. Moreover, success factors as well as key challenges of German small and medium-sized companies are presented. Finally, the result if the consulted companies would invest in India again is provided.

Tariff barriers are hard to overcome. Nevertheless, German companies should constantly read up on the Indian tax system to avoid payments of additional charges.

In relation to non-tariff barriers, five interviewees stated that the collaboration with Indian authorities can be improved by well-established networks of contacts. The resulting issues can be reduced if the appropriate contact person is known. In addition, consultants can take over administrative formalities as they are well versed in authorities.[352] In relation to contracts, the managing director of a lawyer's office suggested inserting all eventualities to avoid subsequent disputes.[353]

For reducing market-related barriers, small and medium-sized companies should conduct an environmental analyse to diminish resulted impediments.

Moreover, foreign investors should think about operations in the so-called SEZ's as they can benefit from improved electrical power supply and infrastructural facili-

[350] Cf.: Appendix, Interview 4, p. LX; Interview 5, p. LXIV.
[351] Cf.: Appendix 2, p. XVIII.
[352] Cf.: Appendix 3, Interview 1, p. LII; Interview 3, p. LVII; Interview 7, p. LXX; Interview 8, p. LXXII; Interview 9, p. LXXIII.
[353] Cf.: Appendix 3, Interview 12, p. LXXXII.

ties.[354] The promotion of SEZ entails the formation of so-called clusters in which the economic efficiency is enhanced due to the improved infrastructure as well as low-cost credits and support services of better quality. Additionally, these clusters benefit from information and know-how transfers, sharing of inputs, improved services and technologies as well as from attracting customers and suppliers and increased level of expertise.[355]

In regard of the theme corruption, the managing director of a consultancy company reported that the costs in connection of bribery can be reduced by having well-established networks of contacts.[356]

In conjunction with the reduction of market-related barriers, the managing director of lawyer's office stated that high labour turnovers can be diminished by incentives and additional benefits such as further trainings, cars, mobile phones and insurances.[357] Moreover, further trainings for employees should be considered as the level of training and qualifications is comparatively low.

Furthermore, small and medium-sized companies should be concentrated on domestic customers as the domestic market demand is high.[358]

The mentioned company-related barriers can be reduced by training programs as they ease the understanding of different cultures and are important in international business relationships. Therefore potential issues arising from dealing with international customers, negotiating joint ventures or entering new markets can be diminished. In addition, individual trainings should be conducted as cultural barriers emerge from misunderstandings on the individual level.

In addition, company-related barriers can be minimized with the help of agents and distributors as they represent the company in the host country and have a steady contact to the customers. This can be helpful for example if a subsidiary is not yet built and the manager is in the process of entering a new market. Moreover, agents can act as intermediaries if communication issues arise.[359] Furthermore, institutions and organisations can advise German small and medium-sized companies in relation to their market entry in India whereupon especially the Indo-German Chamber of Commerce is helpful. Additionally, networks are important in Indian as they can ease the minimization of company-related barriers.

---

[354] Cf.: Pilny, K. (2006), p. 50.
[355] Cf.: Das, K. (2007), p. 85 et seq..
[356] Cf.: Appendix 3, Interview 10, p. LXXVII.
[357] Cf.: Appendix 3, Interview 12, p. LXXXII.
[358] Cf.: Appendix 2, p. XVI.
[359] Cf.: McAuley, A. (2001), p. 61 et seqq..

In conjunction with the challenges arising from the personnel recruitment, the managing director of a consultancy company suggested the collaboration with local consultants as they are more familiar with application procedures. Moreover, he reported that companies are supported by the Chamber of Industry and Commerce Abroad in regard of the personnel recruitment.[360]

For overcoming company-related barriers, two consultancy companies recommended the cooperation with an Indian company in the form of a joint venture as the Indian partner is versed in the Indian market and the German company can benefit from the network of the Indian partner.[361] In regard of the collaboration with a local partner, the managing director of a lawyer's office stated that incentives should be provided and personal contacts as well as permanent monitoring are important.[362]

In conjunction with language barriers the managing director of a consultancy company reported even though English is widely spread, the best businesses can be transacted if they regional language is spoken and if the respective business culture is understood.[363]

In relation of the marketing mix, the consulted companies pointed out that product adaptation is required to successfully operate in India. In this regard, interviewees reported that India should be segmented in regional markets due to its huge diversity whereupon market knowledge is essential.[364] Moreover, five of 14 interviewees stated that the product price is more important than its quality. Therefore products do not have to be over-engineered, but functional and should be purchased at a competitive price.[365]

Additionally, small and medium-sized companies should consider that eligible projects are supported by the bank group Development Loan Corporation (KfW) with the help of long-term loans with low interests if the company turnover is less than Euro 500 million.[366]

---

[360] Cf.: Appendix 3, Interview 5, p. LXIV.
[361] Cf.: Appendix 3, Interview 1, p. LI; Interview 8, p. LXXII.
[362] Cf.: Appendix 3, Interview 12, p. LXXXII.
[363] Cf.: Appendix 3, Interview 13, p. LXXXV.
[364] Cf.: Appendix 3, Interview 9, p. LXXIII; Interview 12, p. LXXXII; Interview 13, p. LXXXV.
[365] Cf.: Appendix 3, Interview 3, p. LVIII; Interview 4, p. LX; Interview 5, p. LXIV; Interview 7, p. LXX; Interview 14, p. LXXXVIII.
[366] Cf.: Waldkirch, K. (2006), p. 108.

According to the questionnaire respondents, the most important factors to successfully manage a company in India are patience, networks, ordinary and cost-effective products, faithful management, personnel selection and manpower as well as know-how of the market situation.[367] Less monetary and human resources as well as "no name"-products are the key challenges for the consulted small and medium-sized companies in comparison to large concerns in regard of the market entry in India.[368] Furthermore, 70 per cent of the participants mentioned that the lack of contacts is a typical market entry barrier.[369] Moreover, 50 per cent of the interviewees reported that patience and sufficient temporal resources are important to enter the Indian market.[370] Additionally, sufficient financial and appropriate human resources are essential according to the managing director of a consultancy company.[371]

However, small and medium-sized companies benefit from flexible reactions to market behaviour, tax reductions and short decision making processes according to the questionnaire respondents.[372]

Concluding, 80 per cent of the participating companies stated that they would invest in India. The most mentioned reason for this evaluation is India's good market potential.[373]

---

[367] Cf.: Appendix 2, p. XLIII.
[368] Cf.: Appendix 2, p. XLIV.
[369] Cf.: Appendix 2, p. XLVI.
[370] Cf.: Appendix 3, Interview 2, p. LII; Interview 6, p. LXVIII; Interview 8, p. LXXI; Interview 9, p. LXXIV; Interview 10, p. LXXVII; Interview 11, p. LXXIX; Interview 12, p. LXXXII.
[371] Cf.: Appendix 3, Interview 8, p. LXXI.
[372] Cf.: Appendix 2, p. XLV.
[373] Cf.: Appendix 2, p. XLVII.

6. Conclusion

Summarized, fundamental factors of success for a market entry in India are comprehension for the Indian structures and market, competitive prices, product adaptation to Indian customer requests, sufficient managerial capacities, networking, enough power of endurance and patient as well as qualified employees in regard of qualification, internationality and loyalty.

In comparison to large companies, small and medium-sized companies often have fewer financial and human resources thus the capacity for international activities is higher for bigger firms. Therefore economies of scale can be easier achieved by large concerns. On the contrary, smaller firms can often react more flexible on market changes. Frequently, small and medium-sized companies are able to create specialized niche products and thus satisfy customer needs. In addition, they are more adaptable and cost-effective in regard of shortened product life cycles and changing consumer tastes as they are more customer-orientated.

6.1. Target achievement

The information provided for German small and medium-sized companies should be censored as in total 40 questionnaires and 14 interviews were analyzable. Consequently, these findings should be seen as a guideline for German investors whereupon the results presented in the literature should be additionally considered and further impediments can exacerbate the market entry in India. Therefore the presented findings do not constitute a conclusive result and further researches are conceivable.

In this study the most important market entry barriers for German small and medium-sized companies have been identified with the help of the conducted surveys in the form of questionnaires and interviews. Based on these findings most of the impediments result from market-related conditions.

The most important tariff and non-tariff barriers for German small and medium-sized companies are connected with the Indian tax system and the high bureaucracy. In relation to the market-related barriers, investors should consider that they vary dependent on the respective location thus the choice of location should be advisedly done to avoid preventable impediments. The most influential criteria in conjunction with market-related barriers are corresponding to the quality of the local public and national transportation routes, corruption, postal system, property market, electricity and water supply, the employees' level of training and qualification as well as environmental conditions according. In regard to company-related barriers, for small and medium-sized companies challenges are posed by the Indian work ethic, caste system, importance of family, different perception of time, collaboration with service providers and the high price elasticity.

The identified market entry barriers for small and medium-sized companies are consistent with those impediments mentioned in the literature for large concerns in regard of bureaucracy, corruption, caste system, import regulations, labour force, tariffs and taxes as well as the Indian mentality and diversity. Comparatively, the insufficient infrastructure is not considered as an important barrier for small and medium-sized companies. Additionally, the consulted companies are impeded by the postal system, property market, electricity and water supply, environmental conditions different perception of time, collaboration with service providers and the high price elasticity.

6.2 Prospects

For future market entrance of small and medium-sized companies in India, impediments can be reduced or even overcome, if companies have well-established networks of contacts and sufficient resources, pay attention to details, are focused on customer services and are flexible as well as patient.

Reforms of the tax system, import regulations and labour law would raise foreign direct investments and more German small and medium-sized would be attracted to invest in India.

India can serve as a stepping stone in further emerging countries for German small and medium-sized companies. A strategic basis for future competitive advantages can be created as German companies can participate in setting the Indian market structures and standards.

To sum up, almost all patient German companies are successfully established in India and give an account of good businesses which they did not anticipate at the beginning of their engagement in India.

Index of appendixes

Appendix 1) Designed questionnaire

FOM Hochschule für Oekonomie & Management University of Applied Sciences

Questionnaire to bachelor thesis:

Market entry barriers for German small and medium-sized companies in India

In preparation for my bachelor thesis I would like to ask you to fill out this questionnaire. Due to the lack of secondary sources you will assist me in procuring data by answering this questionnaire.

Please note:
All data will be treated confidentially and will only be used for statistical purposes. Company-related data will be destroyed upon the completion of my bachelor thesis.

You will be able to rate the different criteria on scales ranging 1 - 4. Additional comments or remarks can be made at the end of this questionnaire.

I am very grateful for your assistance with this questionnaire and in doing so helping me to prepare my bachelor thesis.

Thank you and kind regards,

Diana Bednarek (nee Hellwig)

Contact:	Diana Bednarek
Phone:	+49 176-23546951
Email:	diana.bednarek@gmx.de

Company name:

Industrial sector:

Contact person:

Phone:

Email:

Company size: app. Employees; app. EUR annual turnover

Company location(s) in India:

Year of commencement of operations:

Number of employees in India:

The operation your answers relate to is

- ☐ A wholly-owned subsidiary
- ☐ An administrative branch
- ☐ The headquarters of a joint venture
- ☐ An agency / a branch
- ☐ A production site
- ☐ Others:

Labour market

1) How would you rate the following criteria in India?
(1 = Very good, 2 = Good, 3 = Bad, 4 = Very bad)

	1	2	3	4
a. Availability of manpower	☐	☐	☐	☐
b. Level of training / qualifications	☐	☐	☐	☐
c. Labour / wage costs	☐	☐	☐	☐
d. Work ethic (punctuality, sickness absence, loyalty to the company)	☐	☐	☐	☐

Business market

1) How would you rate the following criteria in India?
(1 = Very high, 2 = High, 3 = Low, 4 = Very low)

	1	2	3	4
a. Purchasing power of the market / customers	☐	☐	☐	☐
b. Domestic market demand	☐	☐	☐	☐
c. Quantity (number) of customers	☐	☐	☐	☐
d. Quality of customers (e.g. payment behaviour)	☐	☐	☐	☐
e. Revenue / profits	☐	☐	☐	☐
f. Market potential	☐	☐	☐	☐

Economic climate

1) How would you rate the following criteria in India?
(1 = Very good, 2 = Good, 3 = Bad, 4 = Very bad)

	1	2	3	4
a. Economic climate in general	☐	☐	☐	☐
b. Cooperation with ...				
i. other companies	☐	☐	☐	☐
ii. service providers	☐	☐	☐	☐
iii. public administrations / authorities	☐	☐	☐	☐
iv. policy-makers	☐	☐	☐	☐
v. financial institutions (e.g. banks)	☐	☐	☐	☐
c. Political stability	☐	☐	☐	☐

2) What is your perception of the prevalence of corruption in India?

☐ Very high
☐ High
☐ Low
☐ Very low

3) Have you ever been requested to pay a bribe?

Yes ☐ No ☐

4) In which of the following sectors is bribery especially prevalent in your opinion?

- ☐ Public administration / authorities
- ☐ Banks
- ☐ Politics
- ☐ Relations with other companies (e.g. suppliers, service providers)
- ☐ Others:

5) How would you rate the management effort when dealing with authorities and government officials in India? (Bureaucracy)

- ☐ Very high
- ☐ High
- ☐ Low
- ☐ Very low

Infrastructure

1) How would you rate the **availability** of the following criteria in India?
(1 = Very high, 2 = High, 3 = Low, 4 = Very low)

	1	2	3	4
a. Local public transportation routes (Rail and road traffic, busses, taxis)	☐	☐	☐	☐
b. National transportation routes (Rail and road traffic, shipping, air traffic)	☐	☐	☐	☐
c. International transportation routes (Shipping, air traffic)	☐	☐	☐	☐
d. Electricity supply	☐	☐	☐	☐
e. Water supply	☐	☐	☐	☐
f. Communication systems				
i. Phone / fax	☐	☐	☐	☐
ii. Internet / email	☐	☐	☐	☐
iii. Postal system	☐	☐	☐	☐
g. Sites, building land	☐	☐	☐	☐
h. Buildings	☐	☐	☐	☐
i. Office space	☐	☐	☐	☐

2) How would you rate the **quality** of the following criteria in India?
(1 = Very good, 2 = Good, 3 = Bad, 4 = Very bad)

	1	2	3	4
a. Local public transportation routes (Rail and road traffic, busses, taxis)	☐	☐	☐	☐
b. National transportation routes (Rail and road traffic, shipping, air traffic)	☐	☐	☐	☐
c. International transportation routes (Shipping, air traffic)	☐	☐	☐	☐
d. Electricity supply	☐	☐	☐	☐
e. Water supply	☐	☐	☐	☐
f. Communication systems				
i. Phone / fax	☐	☐	☐	☐
ii. Internet / email	☐	☐	☐	☐
iii. Postal system	☐	☐	☐	☐
g. Sites, building land	☐	☐	☐	☐
h. Buildings	☐	☐	☐	☐
i. Office space	☐	☐	☐	☐

Costs

1) How satisfied are you with the **costs** of the following criteria in India?
(1 = Very satisfied, 2 = Satisfied, 3 = Dissatisfied, 4 = Very dissatisfied)

	1	2	3	4
a. General operating costs	☐	☐	☐	☐
b. Wage / labour costs	☐	☐	☐	☐
c. Non-wage labour costs	☐	☐	☐	☐
d. Rents / site costs	☐	☐	☐	☐
e. Taxes and charges	☐	☐	☐	☐
f. Costs of…				
i. transport	☐	☐	☐	☐
ii. water / electricity	☐	☐	☐	☐
g. Raw materials / upstream products	☐	☐	☐	☐

Standard of life

1) How would you rate the following points pertaining to the **standard of living** in India?
(1 = Very good, 2 = Good, 3 = Bad, 4 = Very bad)

	1	2	3	4
a. Availability of flats / houses	☐	☐	☐	☐
b. Health care	☐	☐	☐	☐
c. Security	☐	☐	☐	☐
d. Climate	☐	☐	☐	☐
e. Environment	☐	☐	☐	☐

General

1) Name the four most important factors which are crucial to run a company successfully in the Indian market in your view.

1.

2.

3.

4.

2) What do you feel differentiates the entry to the Indian market by small and medium-sized enterprises to larger organisations?

3) Are there special benefits for small and medium-sized companies for investing in India? If yes, please name them.

Market entry barriers

1) What are the typical market entry barriers to India's economic framework in your opinion? (check all that apply)

☐ Bureaucracy

☐ Lack of contacts

☐ Competition

☐ Lack of knowledge of the market

☐ Others:

2) What are the typical market entry barriers relating to India's legal framework in your opinion? (check all that apply)

☐ Choice of business type (Ltd.,[1] PLC,[2] Branch Office, Liaison Office, etc.)

☐ Taxes

☐ Property rights (licenses / patents)

☐ Import regulations / customs

☐ Others:

3) What are the typical market entry barriers pertaining to India's social framework in your opinion? (check all that apply)

☐ Religion

☐ Caste system

☐ Importance of family

☐ Others:

4) Which intercultural challenges were you facing after starting your business in India?

Conclusion

1) On the basis of the experiences you had, would you ...

... invest in India again? Yes ☐ No ☐

Please state reasons.

2) What do you consider to be a reasonable company size to enter the Indian market? Please briefly state reasons.

Thank you for your support,
Diana Bednarek

[1] Private Limited Company
[2] Public Limited Company

Appendix 2) Questionnaire evaluation

Operation

1) What kind of operation you have in India?

Wholly-owned subsidiary	Administrative branch	Headquarter of a joint venture	Agency / branch	Production site	Others	n/a
20		3	4	2	10	1

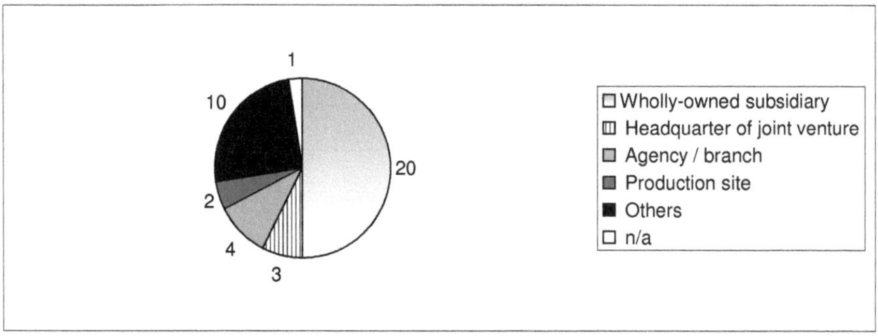

Labour market

1) How would you rate the following criteria in India?

a) Availability of manpower

Very good	Good	Bad	Very bad	n/a
11	21	8		

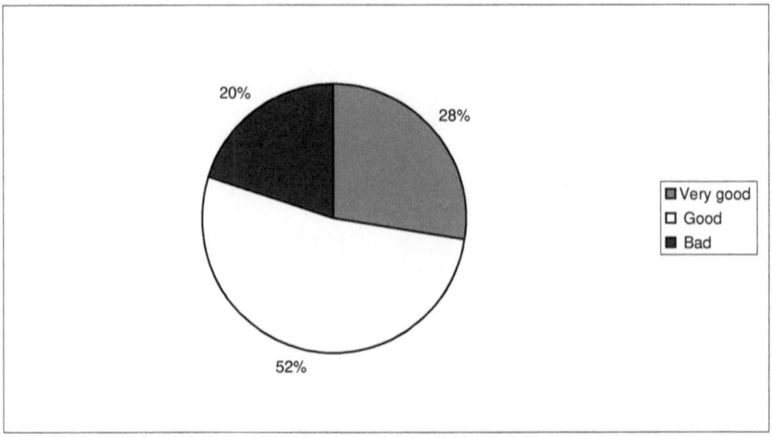

b) Level of training / qualifications

Very good	Good	Bad	Very bad	n/a
4	17	11	8	

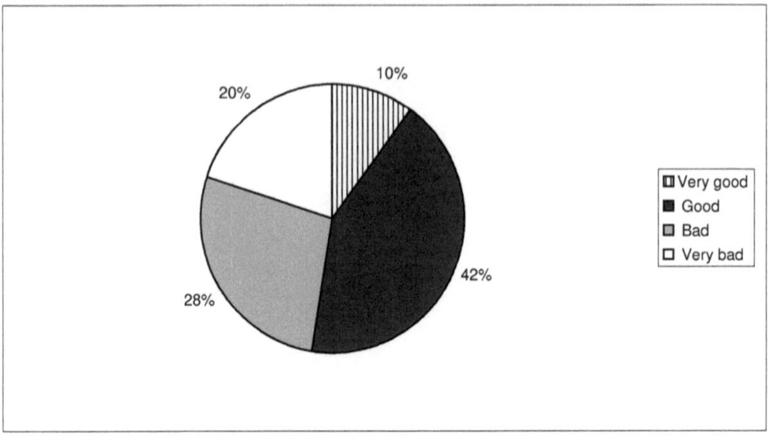

c) Labour / wage costs

Very good	Good	Bad	Very bad	n/a
8	22	9	1	

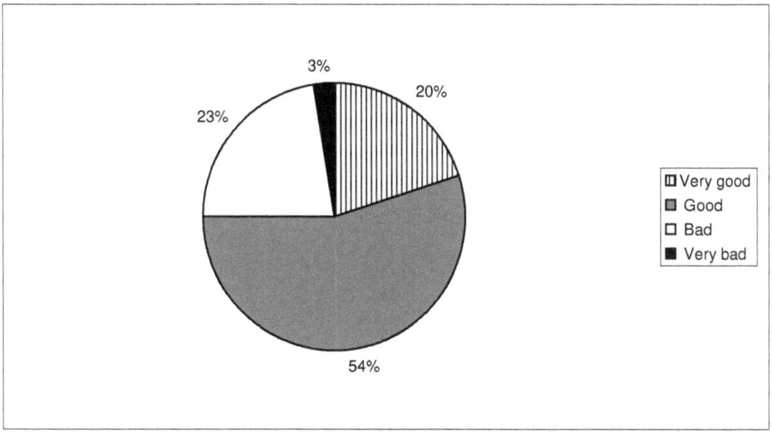

d) Work ethic (punctuality, sickness absence, loyalty to the company)

Very good	Good	Bad	Very bad	n/a
3	11	19	7	

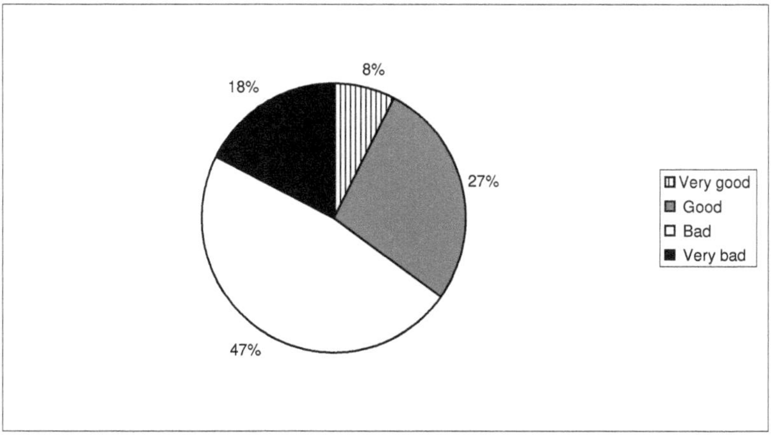

Business market

1) How would you rate the following criteria in India?

a) Purchasing power of the market / customers

Very high	High	Low	Very low	n/a
4	19	12	4	1

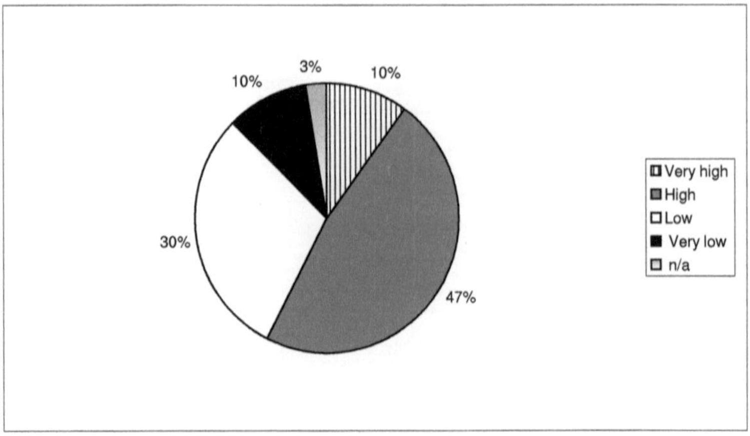

b) Domestic market demand

Very high	High	Low	Very low	n/a
8	24	6	1	1

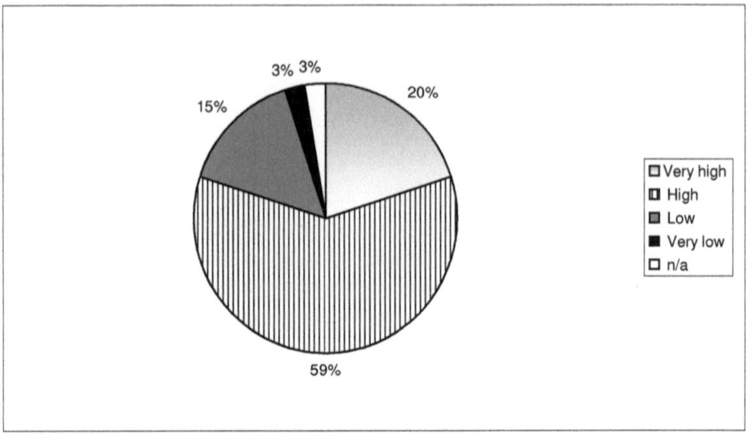

c) Quantity (number) of customers

Very high	High	Low	Very low	n/a
13	16	8	2	1

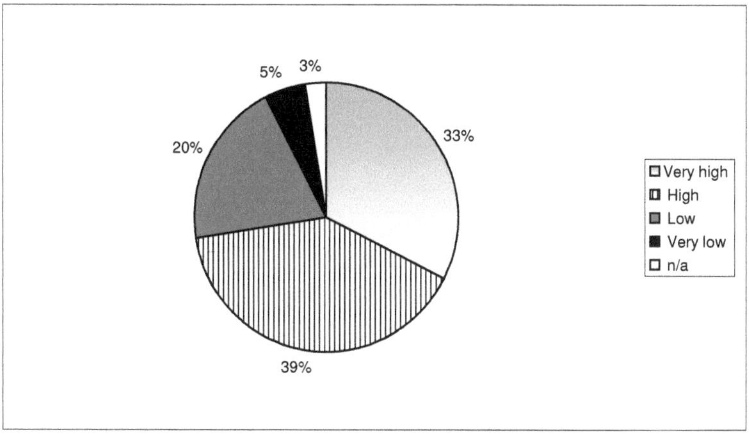

d) Quality of customers (e.g. payment behaviour)

Very high	High	Low	Very low	n/a
2	11	16	9	2

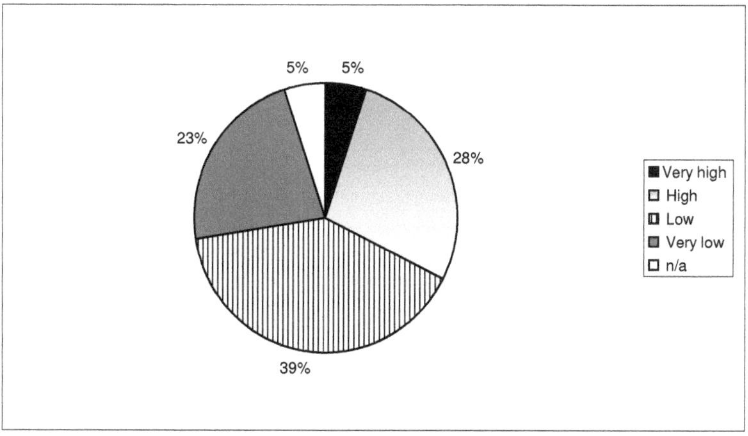

e) Revenue / profits

Very high	High	Low	Very low	n/a
2	14	15	7	2

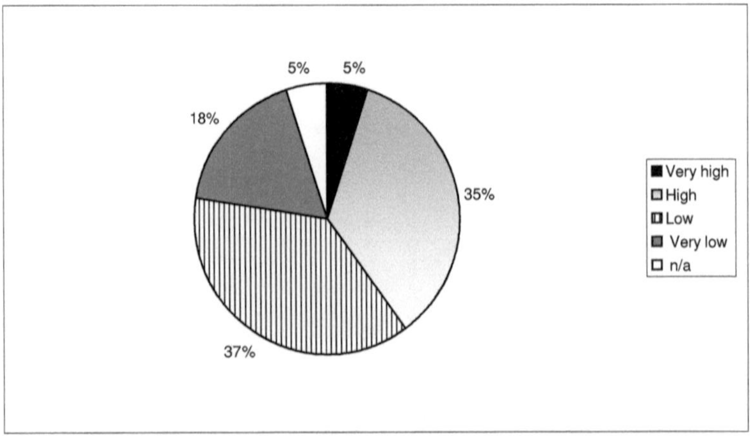

f) Market potential

Very high	High	Low	Very low	n/a
16	21	2		1

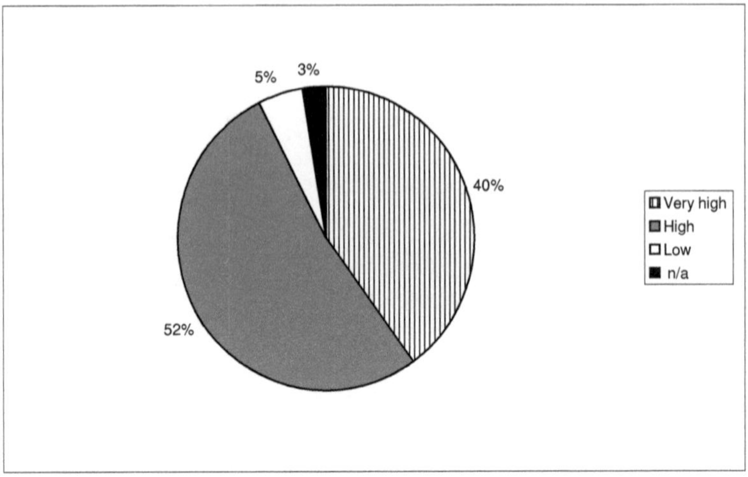

Economic climate

1) How would you rate the following criteria in India?

a) Economic climate in general

Very good	Good	Bad	Very bad	n/a
9	29	2		

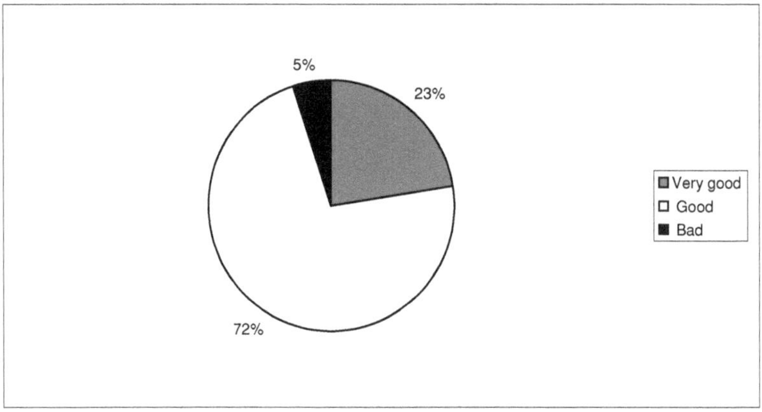

b) I. Cooperation with other companies

Very good	Good	Bad	Very bad	n/a
3	26	8		3

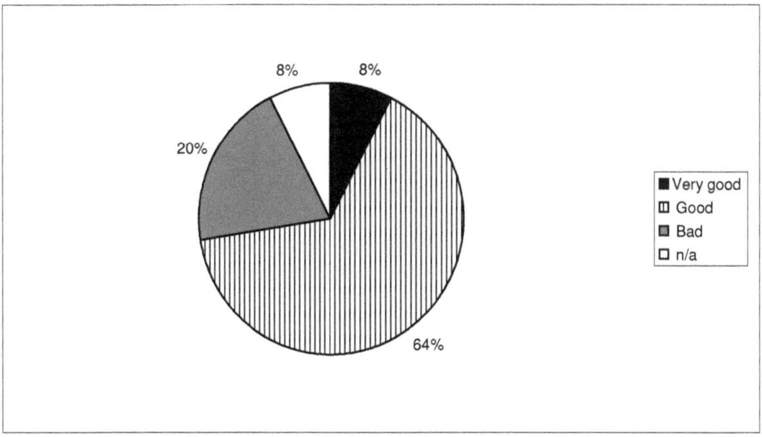

II. Cooperation with service providers

Very good	Good	Bad	Very bad	n/a
3	18	16		3

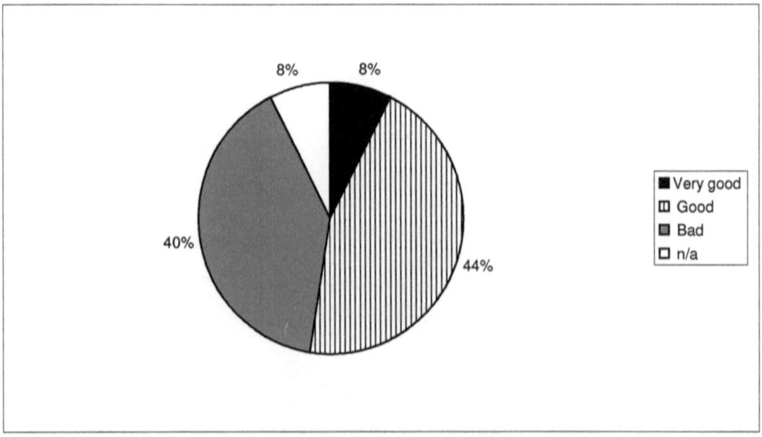

III. Cooperation with public administrations / authorities

Very good	Good	Bad	Very bad	n/a
1		19	18	2

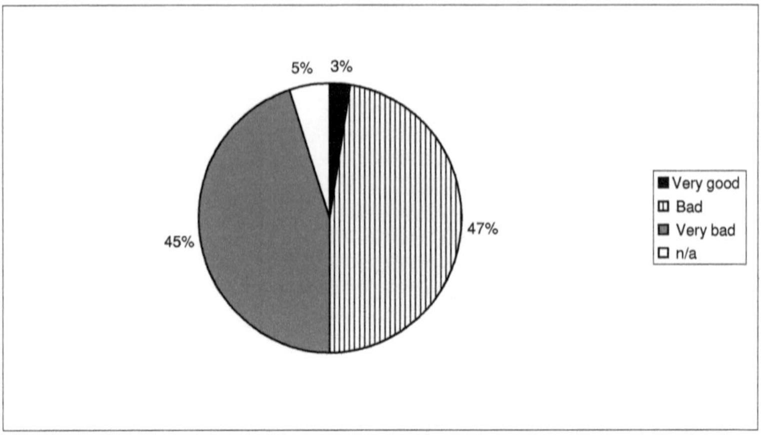

IV. Cooperation with policy-makers

Very good	Good	Bad	Very bad	n/a
	1	24	12	3

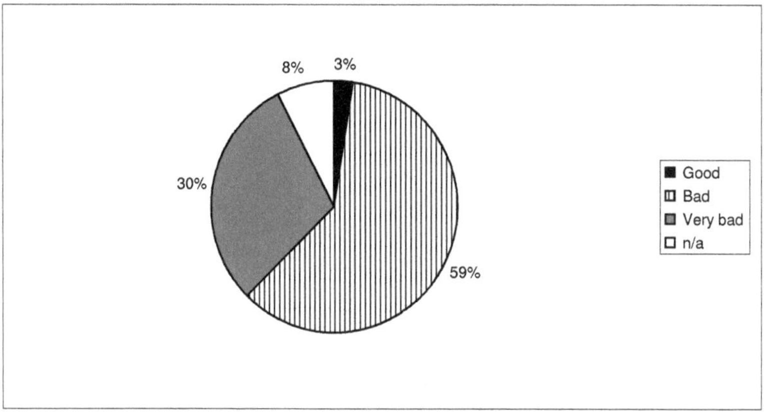

V. Cooperation with financial institutions (e.g. banks)

Very good	Good	Bad	Very bad	n/a
1	12	19	6	2

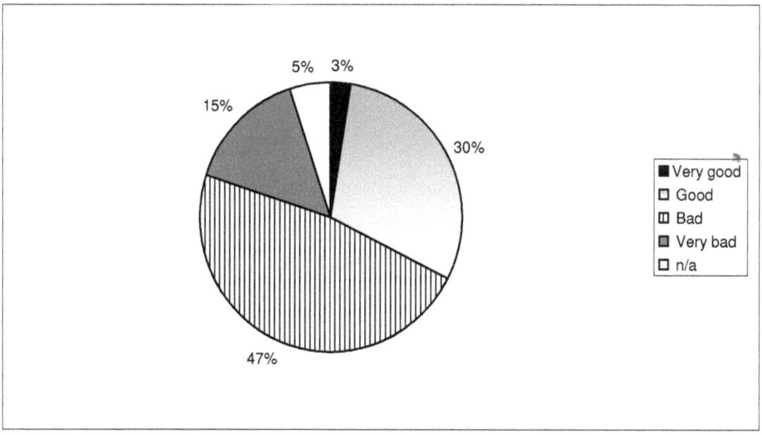

c) Political stability

Very good	Good	Bad	Very bad	n/a
3	22	14		1

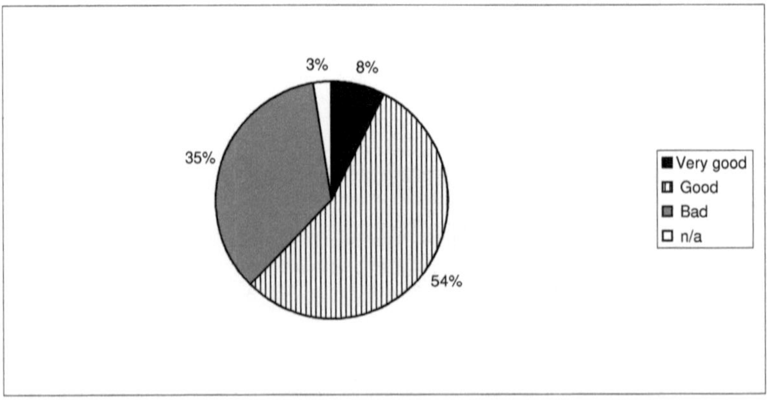

2) What is your perception of the prevalence of corruption in India?

Very high	High	Low	Very low	n/a
14	19	3	1	3

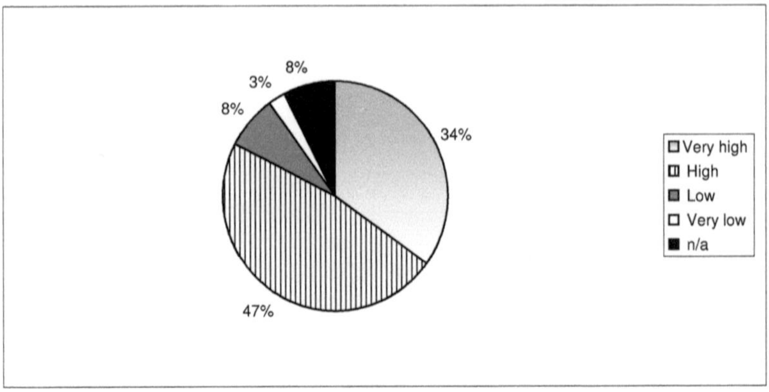

3) Have you ever been requested to pay a bribe?

Yes	No	n/a
15	21	4

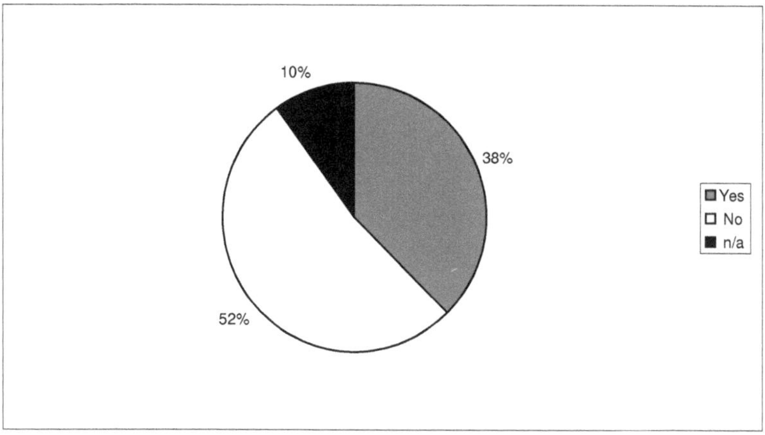

4) In which of the following sectors is bribery especially prevalent in your opinion?

Sectors	Quantity
Public administration / authorities	30
Banks	2
Politics	20
Relations with other companies (e.g. suppliers, service providers)	3
Others	2
n/a	4

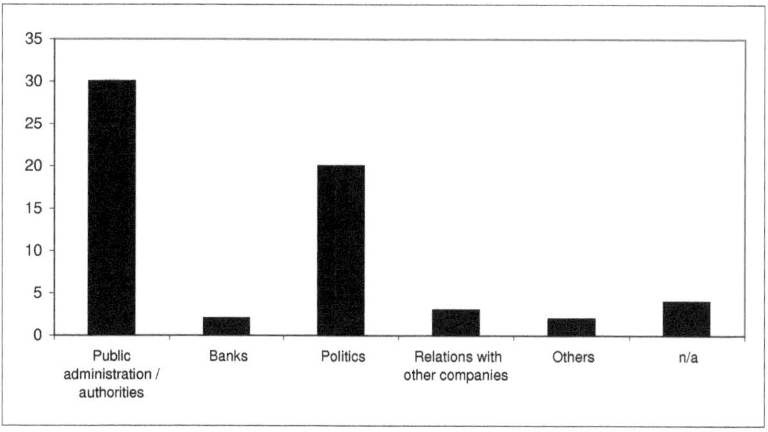

5) How would you rate the management effort when dealing with authorities and government officials in India? (Bureaucracy)

Very high	High	Low	Very low	n/a
20	16	2		2

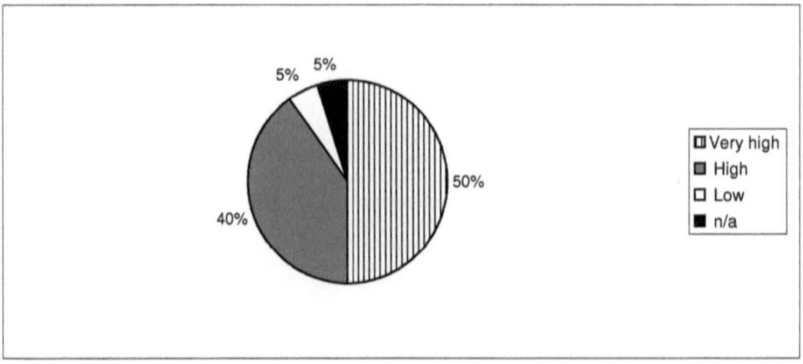

Infrastructure

1) How would you rate the **availability** of the following criteria in India?

a) Local public transportation routes (Rail and road traffic, busses, taxis)

Very high	High	Low	Very low	n/a
3	15	11	9	2

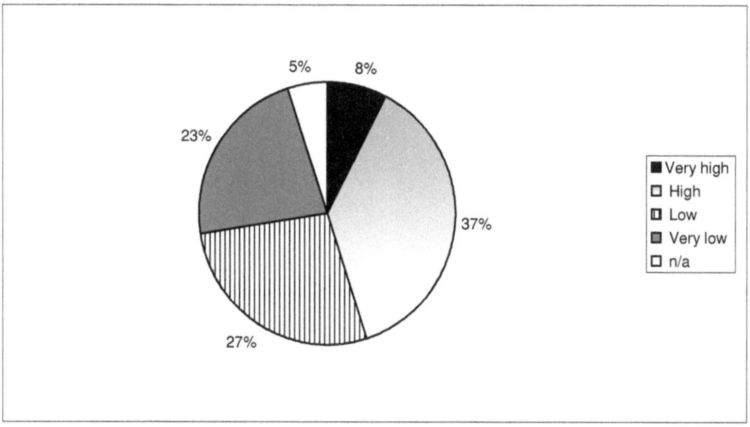

b) National transportation routes (Rail and road traffic, shipping, air traffic)

Very high	High	Low	Very low	n/a
3	18	11	7	1

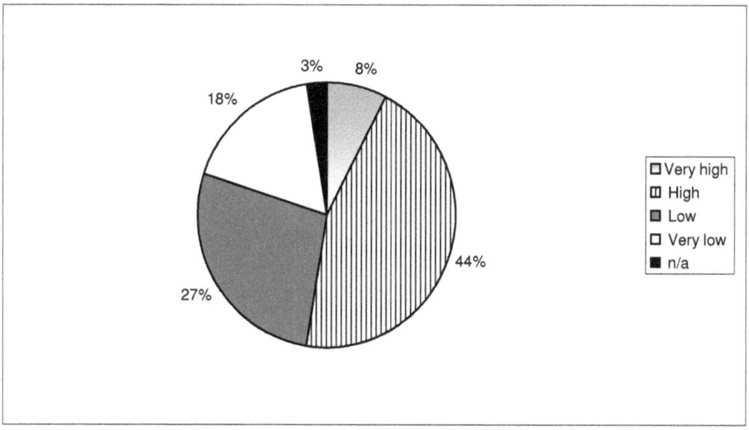

c) International transportation routes (Shipping, air traffic)

Very high	High	Low	Very low	n/a
6	22	11		1

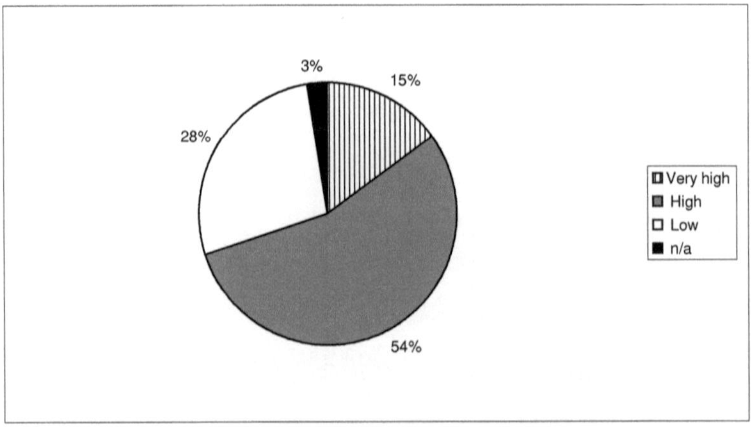

d) Electricity supply

Very high	High	Low	Very low	n/a
	6	24	9	1

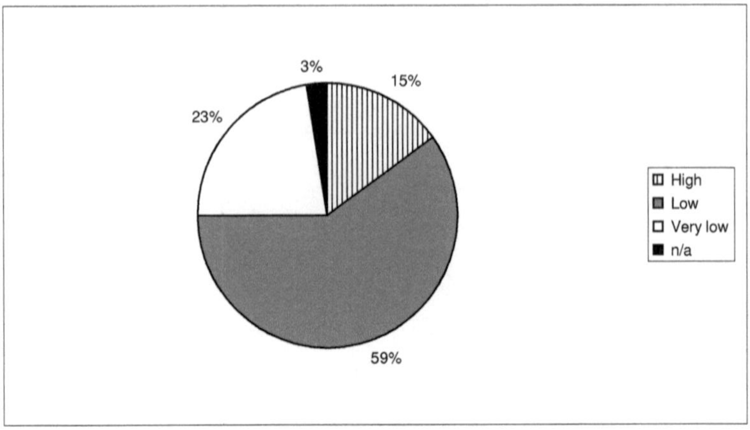

e) Water supply

Very high	High	Low	Very low	n/a
1	12	20	6	1

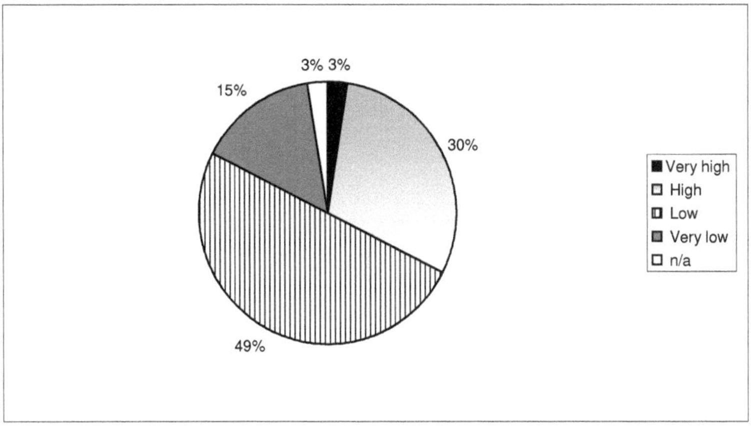

f) Communication systems

I. Phone / fax

Very high	High	Low	Very low	n/a
9	21	9		1

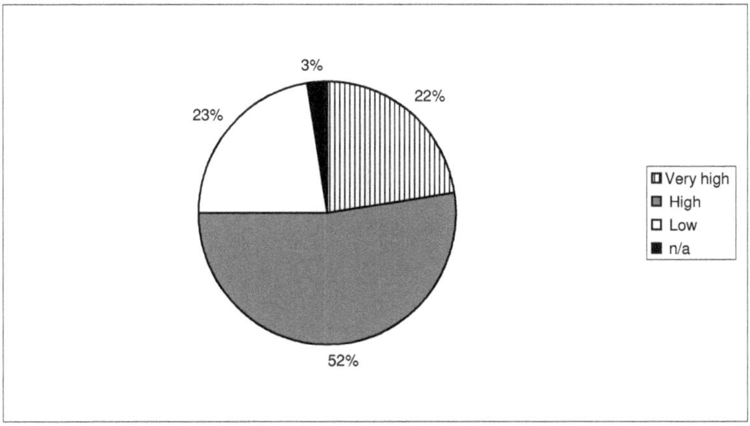

II. Internet / email

Very high	High	Low	Very low	n/a
10	23	5	1	1

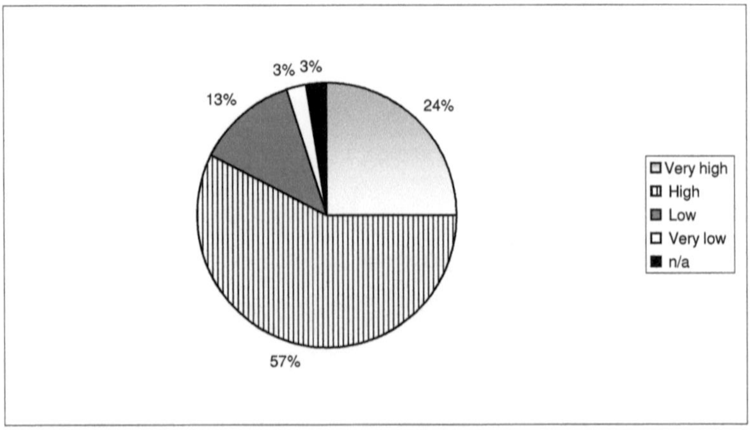

III. Postal system

Very high	High	Low	Very low	n/a
3	18	16	2	1

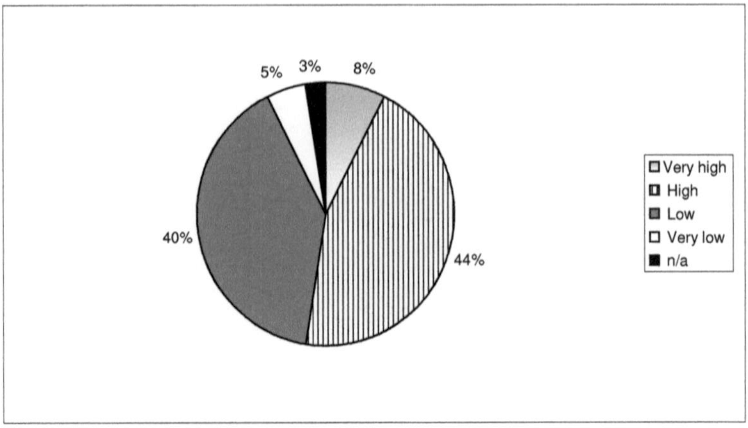

g) Sites, building land

Very high	High	Low	Very low	n/a
5	16	14		5

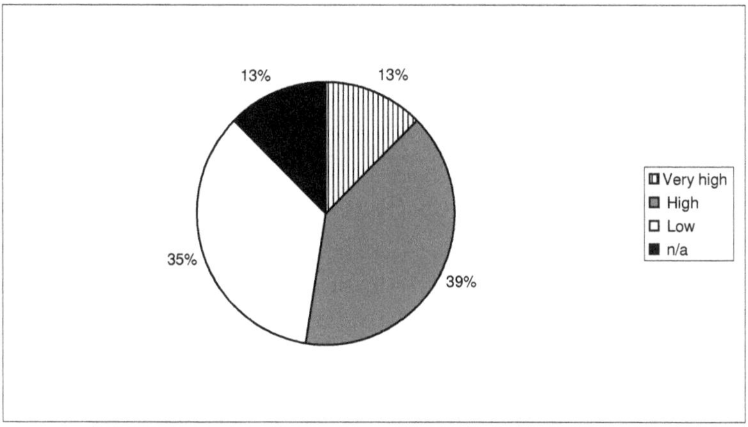

h) Buildings

Very high	High	Low	Very low	n/a
2	15	19	1	3

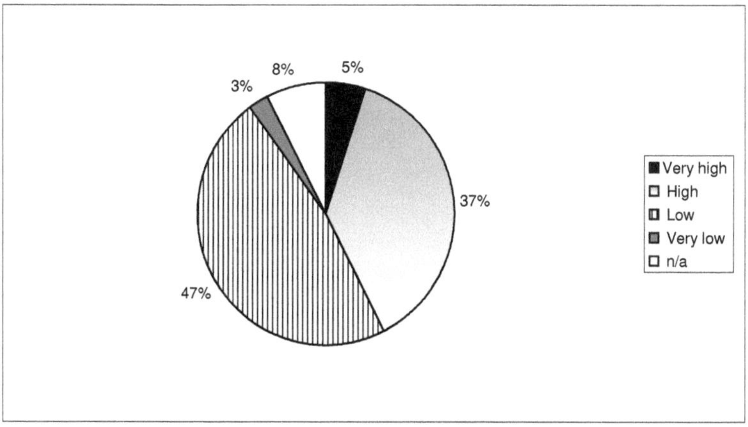

i) Office space

Very high	High	Low	Very low	n/a
1	18	17		4

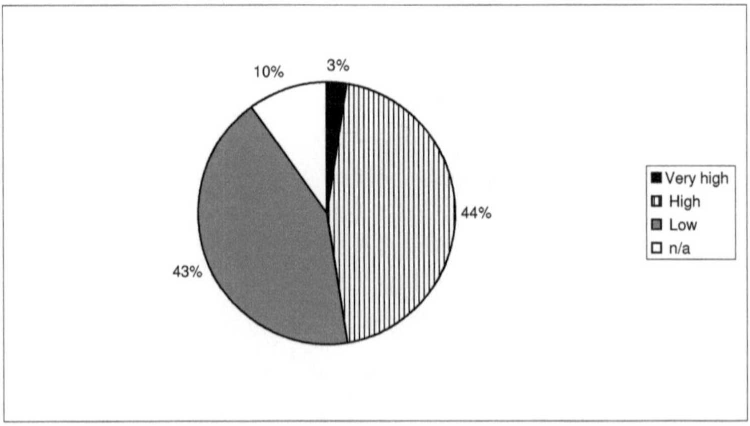

2) How would you rate the **quality** of the following criteria in India?

a) Local public transportation routes (Rail and road traffic, busses, taxis)

Very good	Good	Bad	Very bad	n/a
	8	15	16	1

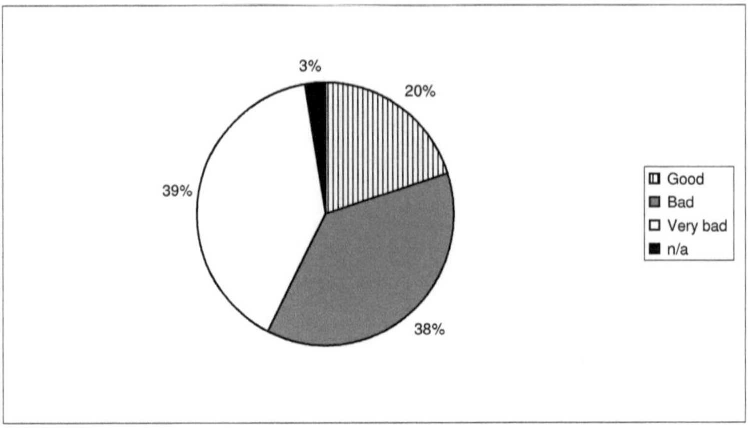

b) National transportation routes (Rail and road traffic, shipping, air traffic)

Very good	Good	Bad	Very bad	n/a
	10	21	8	1

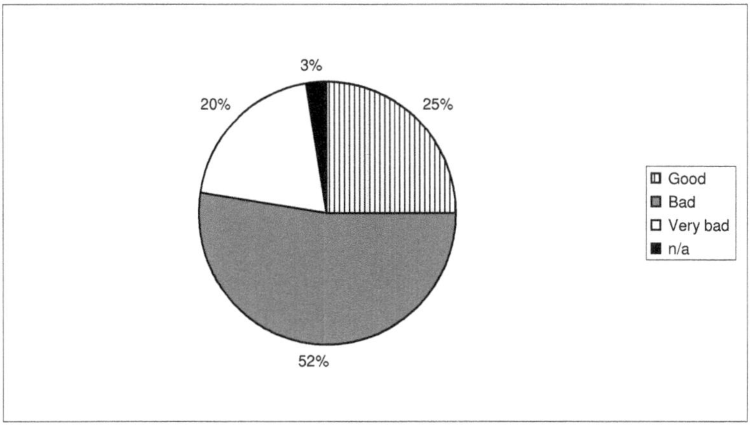

c) International transportation routes (Shipping, air traffic)

Very good	Good	Bad	Very bad	n/a
2	27	10		1

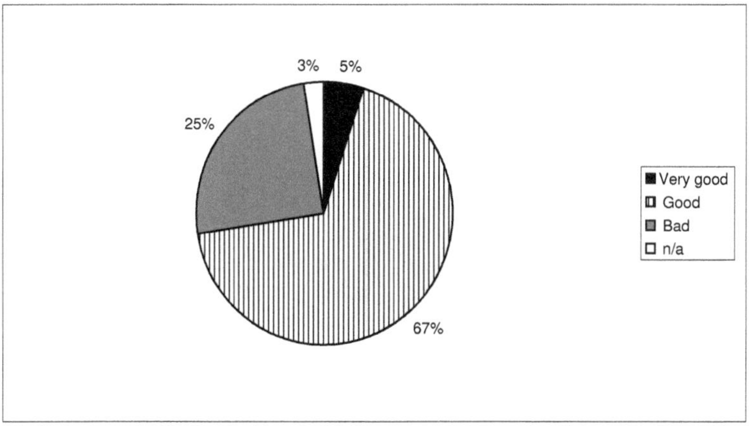

d) Electricity supply

Very good	Good	Bad	Very bad	n/a
	1	24	14	1

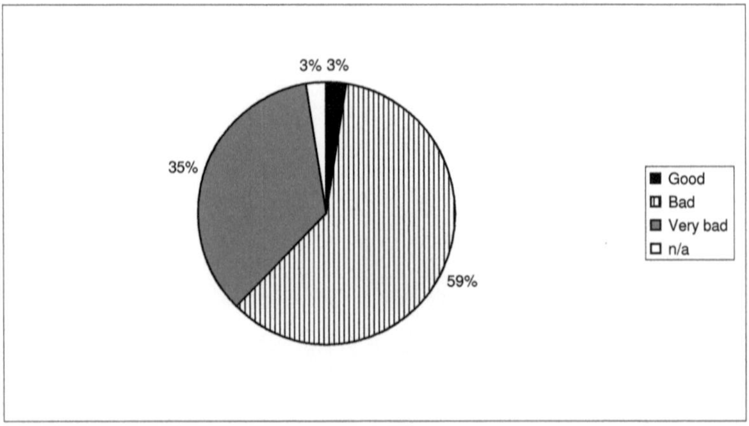

e) Water supply

Very good	Good	Bad	Very bad	n/a
	8	18	13	1

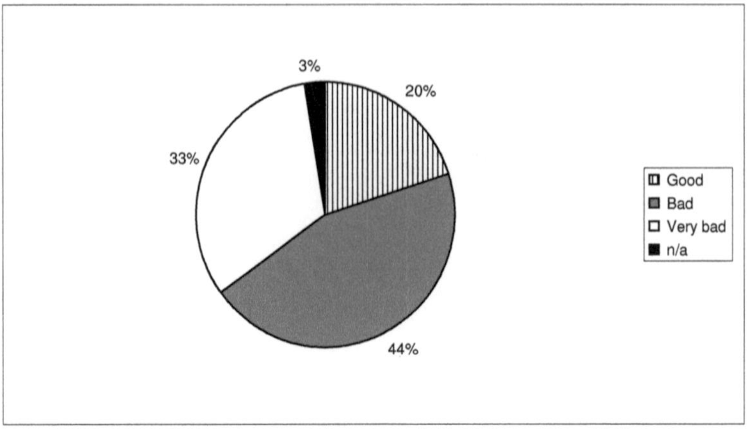

f) Communication systems

I. Phone / fax

Very good	Good	Bad	Very bad	n/a
8	18	10	3	1

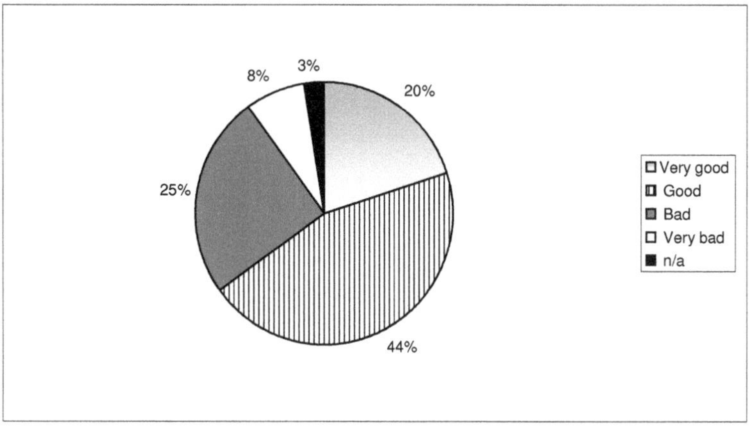

II. Internet / email

Very good	Good	Bad	Very bad	n/a
9	21	8	1	1

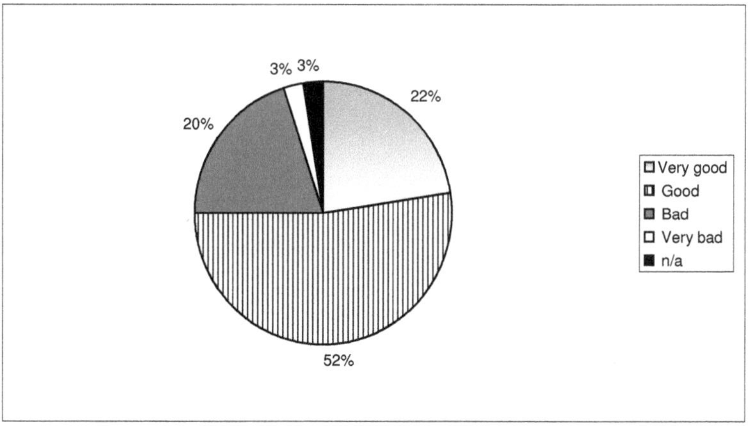

III. Postal system

Very good	Good	Bad	Very bad	n/a
1	12	18	7	2

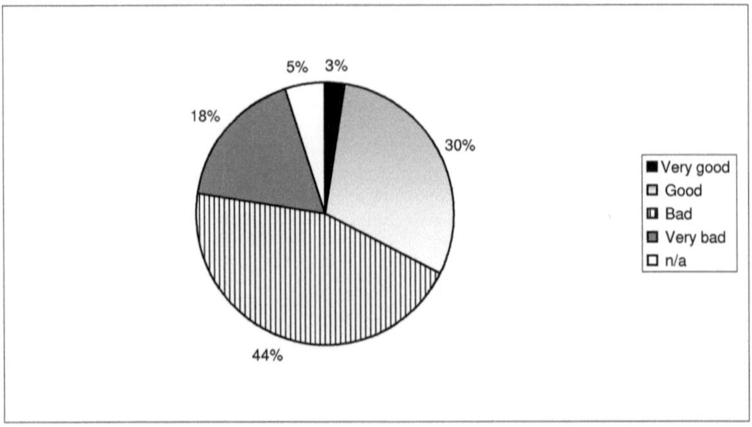

g) Sites, building land

Very good	Good	Bad	Very bad	n/a
1	19	14	3	3

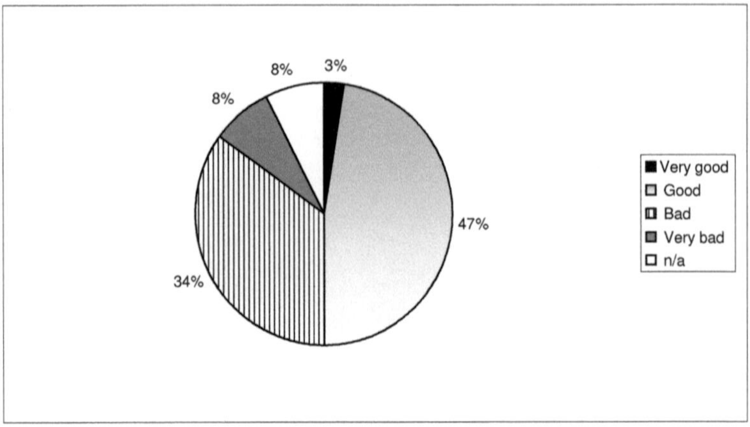

h) Buildings

Very good	Good	Bad	Very bad	n/a
	7	22	7	4

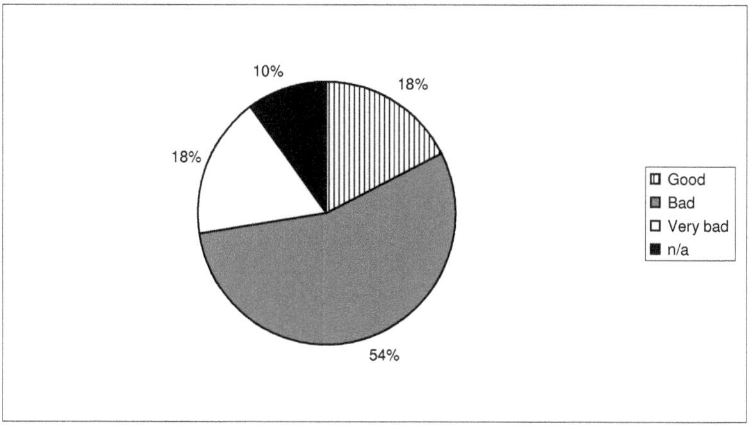

i) Office space

Very good	Good	Bad	Very bad	n/a
1	5	26	5	3

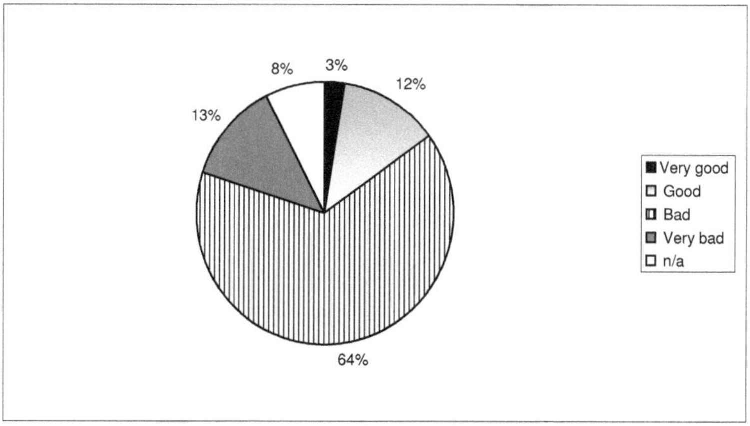

Costs

1) How satisfied are you with the costs of the following criteria in India?

a) General operating costs

Very satisfied	Satisfied	Dissatisfied	Very dissatisfied	n/a
4	22	9	4	2

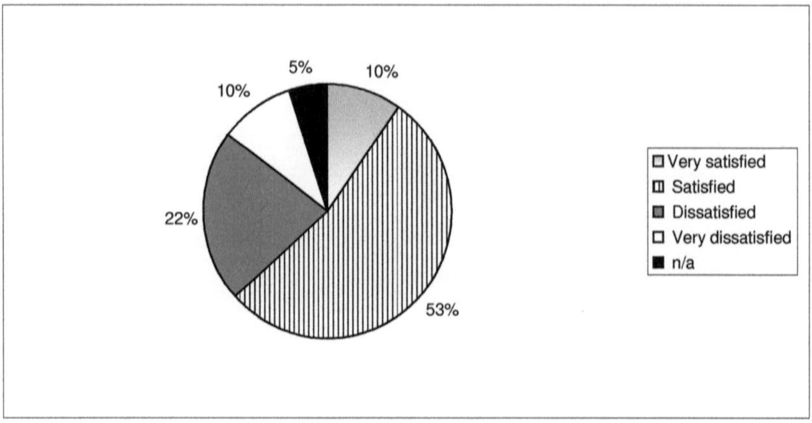

b) Wage / labour costs

Very satisfied	Satisfied	Dissatisfied	Very dissatisfied	n/a
6	25	7		2

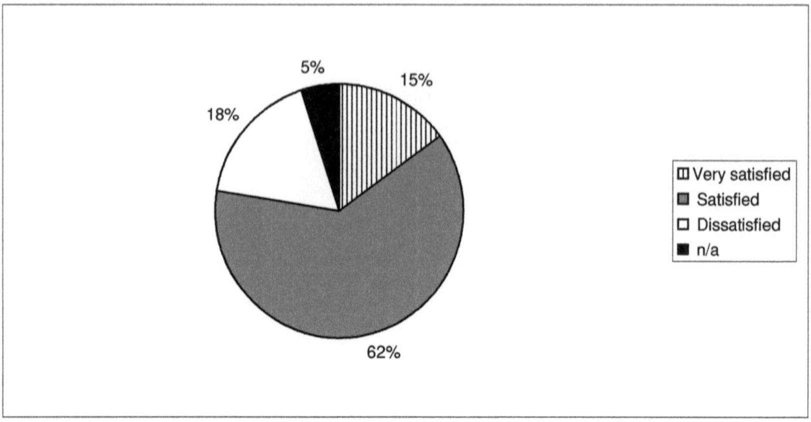

c) Non-wage labour costs

Very satisfied	Satisfied	Dissatisfied	Very dissatisfied	n/a
9	21	5	1	4

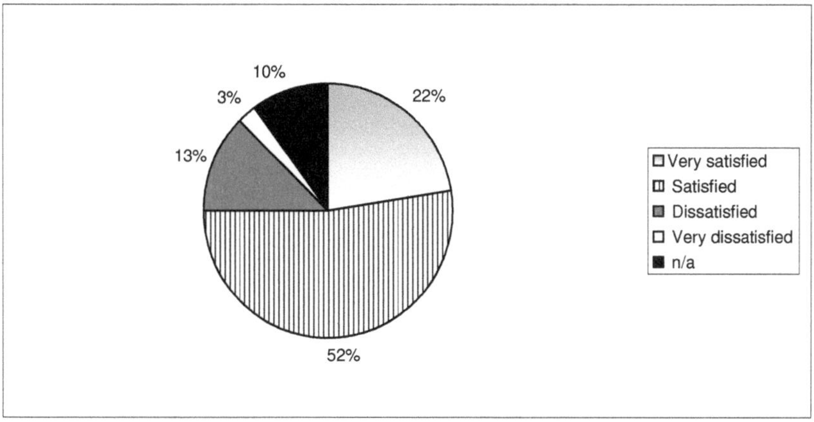

d) Rents / site costs

Very satisfied	Satisfied	Dissatisfied	Very dissatisfied	n/a
2	9	22	4	3

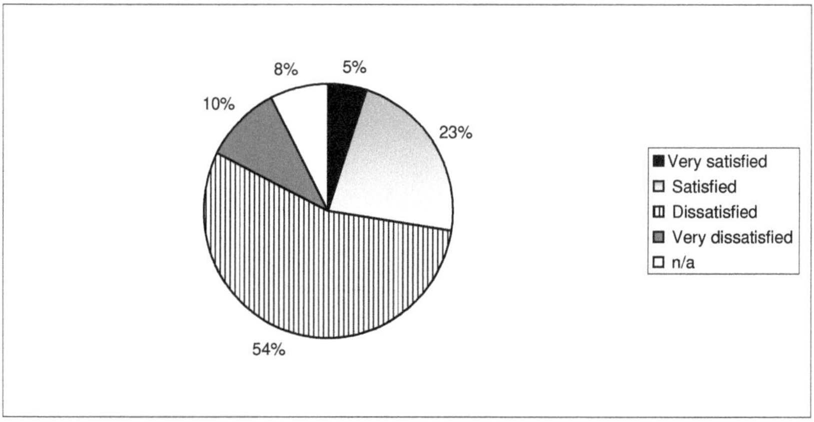

e) Taxes and charges

Very satisfied	Satisfied	Dissatisfied	Very dissatisfied	n/a
1	13	18	3	5

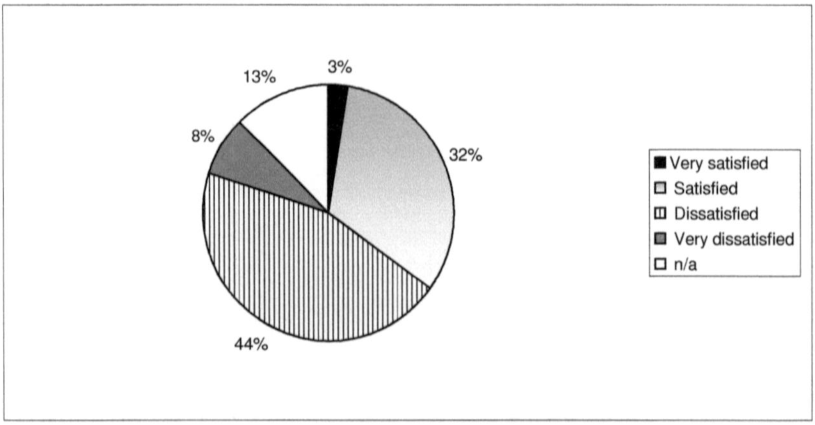

f) Cost of…

I) … transport

Very satisfied	Satisfied	Dissatisfied	Very dissatisfied	n/a
4	25	7	1	3

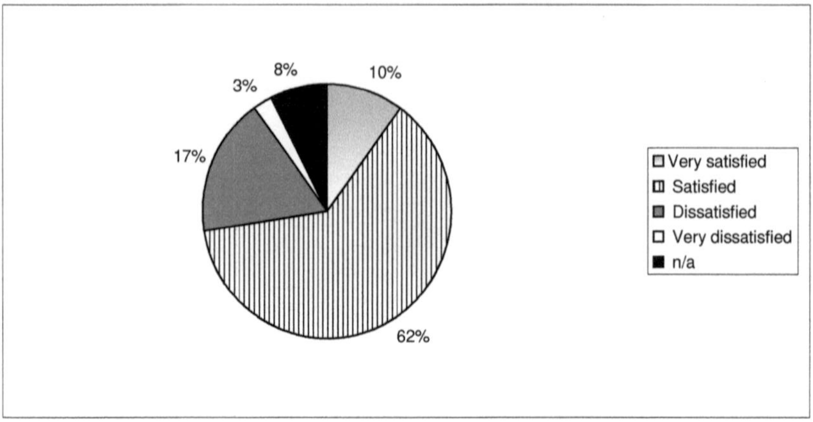

II) ... water / electricity

Very satisfied	Satisfied	Dissatisfied	Very dissatisfied	n/a
1	29	6	1	3

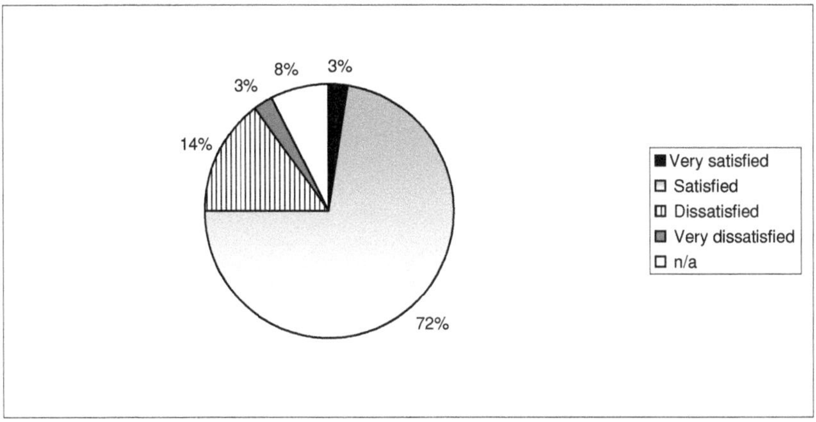

g) Raw materials / upstream products

Very satisfied	Satisfied	Dissatisfied	Very dissatisfied	n/a
1	11	14	2	12

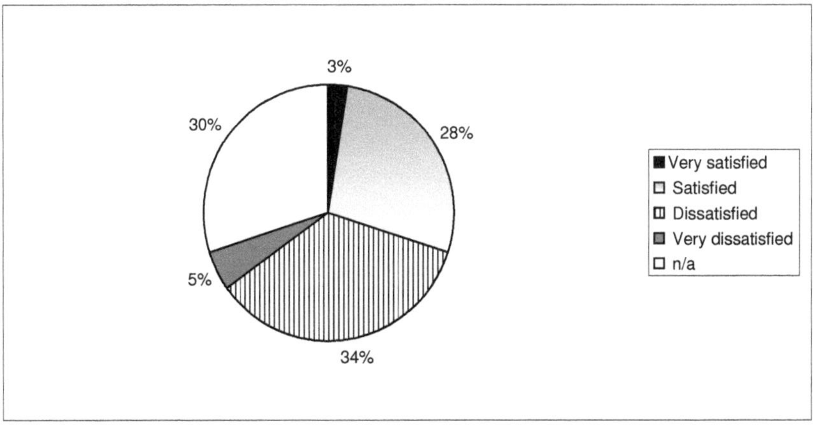

Standard of life

1) How would you rate the following points pertaining to the standard of living in India?

a) Availability of flats / houses

Very good	Good	Bad	Very bad	n/a
3	17	14	3	3

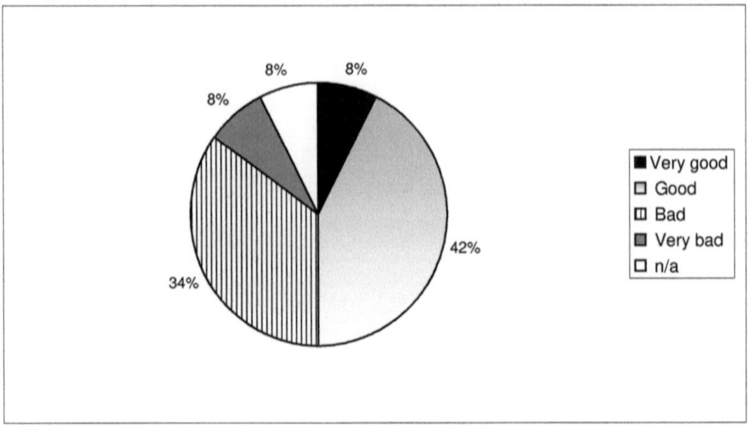

b) Health care

Very good	Good	Bad	Very bad	n/a
2	17	19	2	

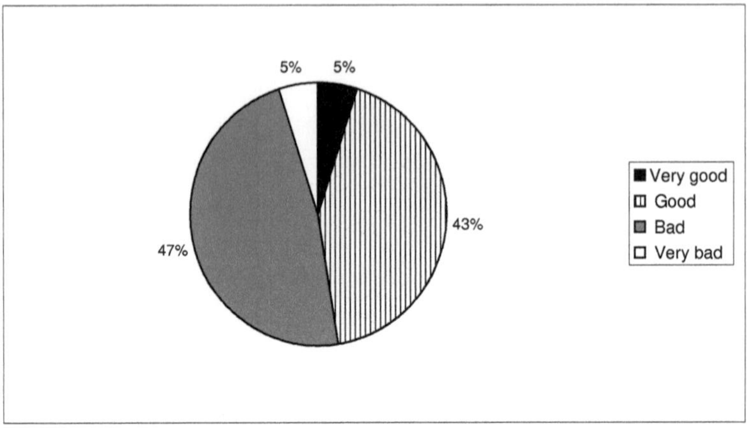

c) Security

Very good	Good	Bad	Very bad	n/a
3	22	13	1	1

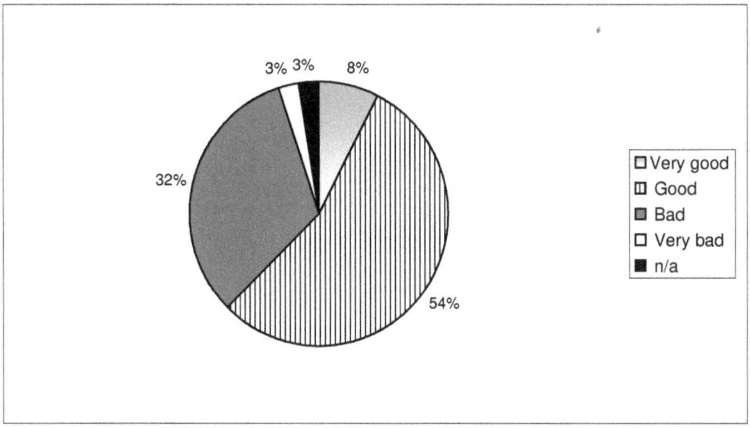

d) Climate

Very good	Good	Bad	Very bad	n/a
2	15	21	2	

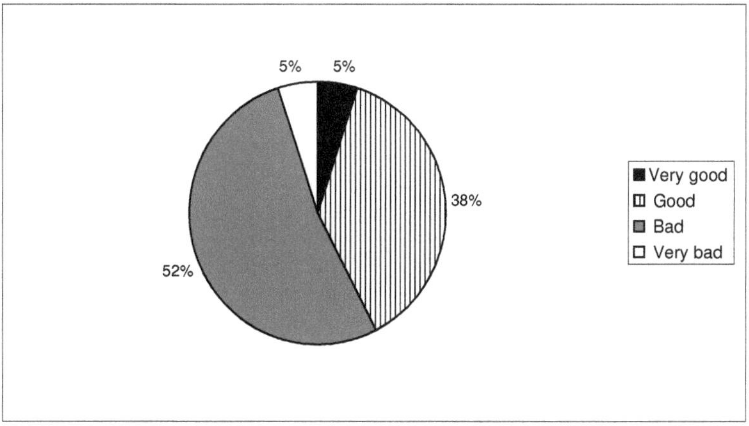

e) Environment

Very good	Good	Bad	Very bad	n/a
	5	13	22	

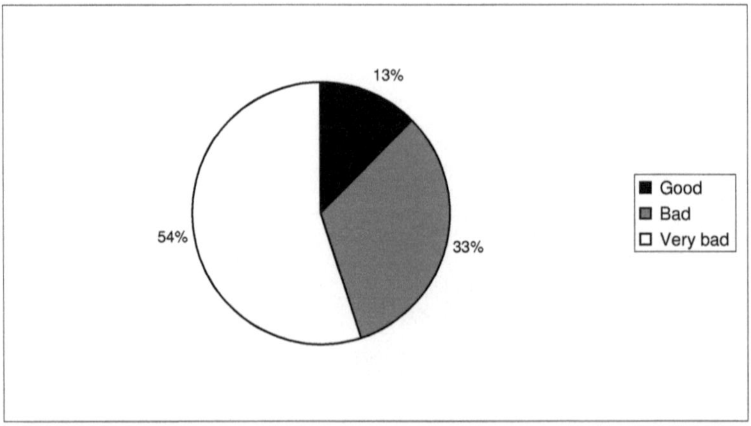

General

1) Name the four most important factors which are crucial to run a company successfully in the Indian market in your view.

	Factors	Quantity
1	Faithful management	9
2	Patient	17
3	Flexibility	5
4	Know-how of the market situation	8
5	Network	17
6	Contact with authorities	1
7	Personnel selection / manpower	9
8	Product quality	2
9	Sufficient capital	2
10	Niche products	1
11	Ordinary and cost-effective products	10
12	Knowledge of the provisions	4
13	Knowledge of the culture	4
14	Communication	3
15	Openness	4
16	Product adaptation	4
17	Proper location	4

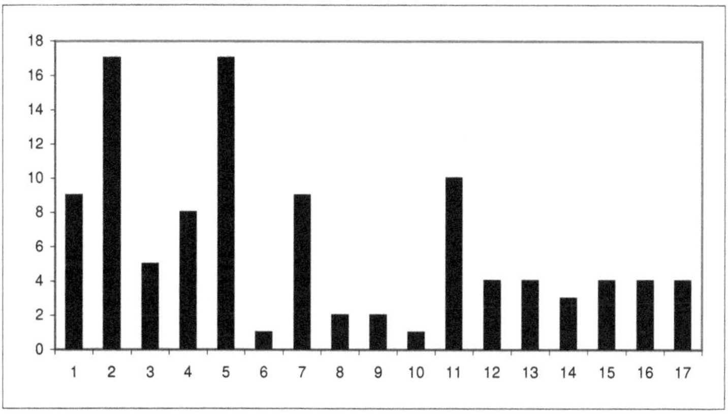

2) What do you feel differentiates the entry to the Indian market by small and medium-sized enterprises to larger organisations?

	Factors	Quantity
1	Challenging contact with cooperation partners	3
2	High competition	2
3	"No name"	5
4	Niche	3
5	Higher flexibility	3
6	Less monetary resources	12
7	High bureaucratic effort	3
8	Less human resources	5
9	No shareholder value	2

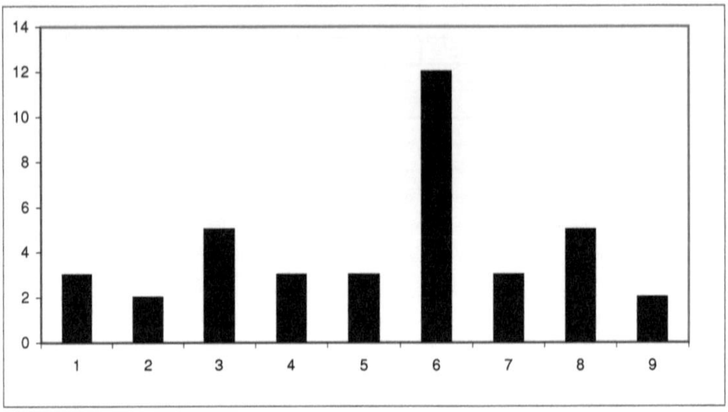

3) Are there special benefits for small and medium-sized companies for investing in India? If yes, please name them.

	Factors	Quantity
1	Dependent on the branch	1
2	Governmental aid	2
3	Tax reduction	5
4	Flexible development of customized products	2
5	Flexible reaction to the market	8
6	Low production costs	1
7	Short decison making process	3
8	Labour law benefits	1

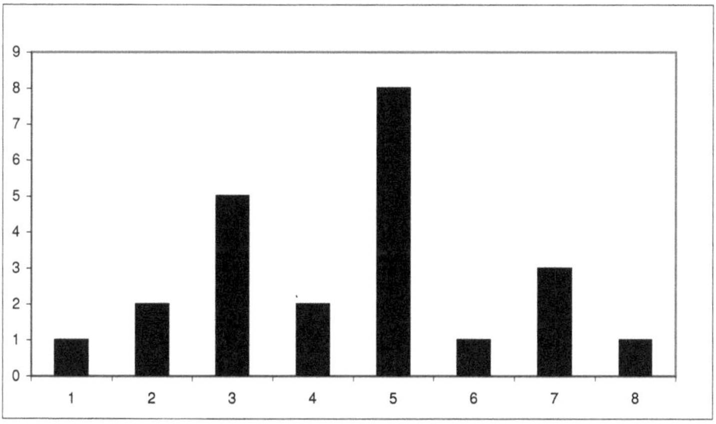

Market entry barriers

1) What are the typical market entry barriers to India's economic framework in your opinion?

Factors	Quantity
Bureaucracy	34
Lack of contacts	28
Competition	4
Lack of knowledge of the market	34

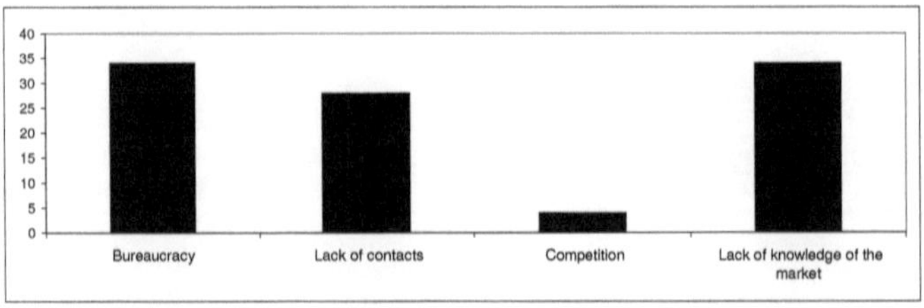

2) What are the typical market entry barriers relating to India's legal framework in your opinion?

Factors	Quantity
Choice of business type	5
Taxes	13
Property rights	6
Import regulations / customs	29

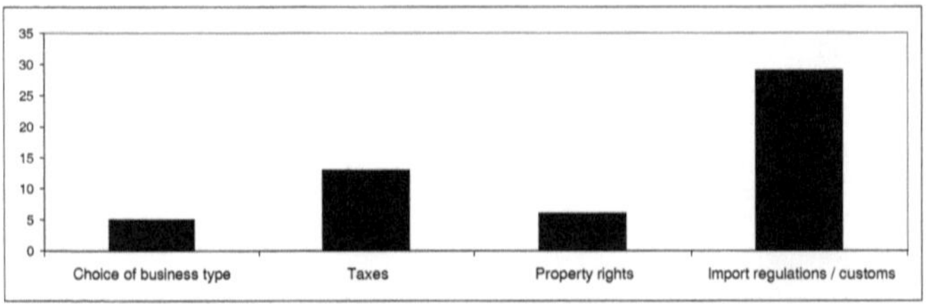

3) What are the typical market entry barriers pertaining to India's social framework in your opinion?

Factors	Quantity
Religion	4
Caste system	11
Importance of family	8

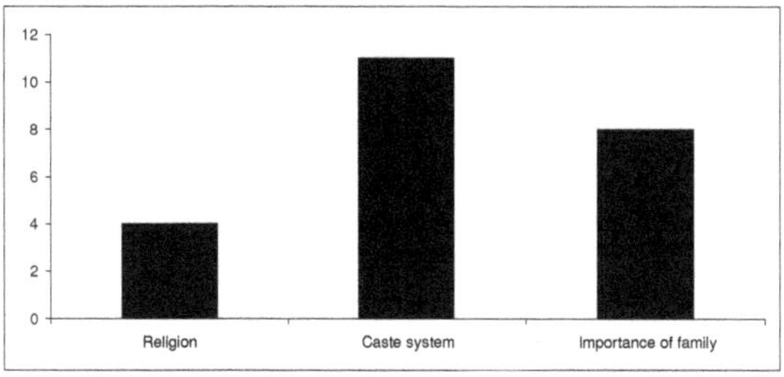

4) Which intercultural challenges were you facing after starting your business in India?

Factors	Quantity
Different perception of time	3
Personel recruitment	1
Job hobbing	1
Language barriers	3
Vacation time	1
Indian management	2
Know how of the Indian mentality	7
High hierarchies	1
Tedious organization of network	2
Religion	2
Local partners	2
Different quality expectations	1

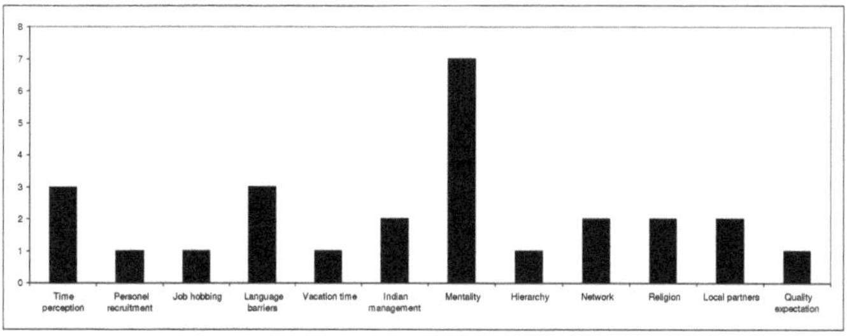

Conclusion

1) On the basis of the experiences you had, would you invest in India again?

Yes	No	n/a
32	6	2

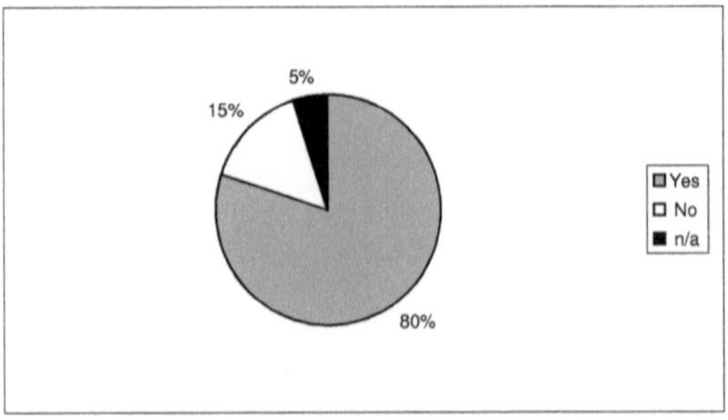

Please state reasons.

YES (Quantity)	Reasons	NO (Quantity)	Reasons
1	High know-how	1	Over-rated purchasing power
1	Low labour costs	2	Costs unequal to benefits
1	Low language barriers	1	Incentive competition
17	Good market opportunity	1	Unrealiability
1	Young and huge populatio	1	Bad payment moral
2	Global presence		

2) What do you consider to be a reasonable company size to enter the Indian market?

Factors	Quantity
Dependent of the product	8
Dependent of the branch	3
Sufficient human resources	3
Sufficient resources for at least three years	2
More than 50 employees	1
Medium to big-sized company	1
Sufficient market potencial	2
Good competitive position	1
Sufficient temporary and financial resources	4
Financial resource for at least one year	1
More than 100 employees	1
Corporate group	2
More than 200 employees	2

Appendix 3) Interviews

Interview 1: Unternehmensberatung

- Datum: 14.02.2012, Uhrzeit: 11:44, Dauer: 33:52 min.
- Interviewpartner: Geschäftsführerin
- Standort: München; Gurgaon
- Unternehmensgröße: 7 Mitarbeiter, davon keine in Indien; circa 1,3 Millionen Euro Jahresumsatz

Das Gespräch folgte einem Leitfaden, wobei einige spezielle Punkte des zuvor ausgefüllten Fragebogens detaillierter beleuchtet wurden.

Zuvor Begrüßung / Small-Talk...

1) **Inwiefern schätzen Sie die Zusammenarbeit mit Behörden, politischen Entscheidungsträgern und Banken als schlecht ein?**

Die Zusammenarbeit ist mit diesen schwierig. Oft versickert das Geld und die Prozesse dauern lange. Die Regeln sind von Behörde zu Behörde unterschiedlich, sodass dies sehr unübersichtlich ist und man ist auf Hilfe von Leuten vor Ort angewiesen. Die Prozesse sind zeitlich nicht absehbar und es dauert alles sehr lang, da es keine fixen Prozesse gibt.

2) **Inwiefern ist aus Ihrer Sicht die Verfügbarkeit der Elektrizitäts- und Wasserversorgung schlecht?**

Es gibt häufig Stromausfälle, bis zu 40 Prozent und daraus resultieren hohe Kosten.

Das Wasser ist dreckig und man sollte niemals Wasser aus dem Hahn trinken. Nur zehn Prozent der indischen Bevölkerung haben einen Zugang zum WC. Es gibt kaum Abwässersysteme oder Kanalisation, sodass alles recht dreckig ist. Gerade Ausländer werden aufgrund der Umweltverhältnisse häufig krank, dies liegt häufig an den auftretenden Bakterien.

3) **Inwiefern ist aus Ihrer Sicht die Qualität der Post schlecht?**

Die Auslieferung der Post kann lange dauern und ist eher unzuverlässig. Oft muss man extra Geld für die Postboten bezahlen, damit die Post zeitnah beziehungsweise überhaupt ausgeliefert wird. In diesem Bereich ist die Korruption stark vertreten. Man weiß nie, ob die Post wirklich ankommt.

4) **Inwiefern ist die Qualität der Gebäude und Räume schlecht?**

Die Gebäude und Räume sind in Indien häufig dreckig und die Qualität ist häufig schlecht.

Gegen die Hitze gibt es keine doppelt verglasten Fenster, nichts ist eben und die Decken sind schief. Häufig werden schlechte Materialien eingesetzt, gegen die Kälte im Winter gibt es keine Heizung und keine Isolation. Kabel hängen von den Decken.
Beim Monsun regnet es durch und häufig schimmelt es. Dabei wird der Schimmel nicht beseitigt, sondern einfach drüber gemalert.
Die Qualitätsansprüche sind in Indien anders als in Deutschland, vieles ist verkommen. Klimaanlagen funktionieren nicht und die Wetterschwankungen sind enorm. Im Winter kann es sehr kalt werden und es ist nass, im Sommer kann es bis zu 50 Grad warm werden. Diese Schwankungen gehen an die Substanz.
Außerdem sind Ratten keine Seltenheit.

5) **Können Sie mir bitte erläutern, wieso Sie mit den Kosten für Miete und Grundstücke unzufrieden sind?**

Die Mieten sind wahnsinnig hoch und dies zu schlechter Qualität. Dies trifft besonders auf Delhi zu, das ein großes Ballungscenter darstellt. Hier werden die Mietpreise von DLF-Immobilien diktiert. Es ist sehr sehr teuer und eng und die Preise steigen weiter, da die Nachfrage sehr hoch ist und viele nach Delhi ziehen wollen. Da es kaum Konkurrenz auf dem Immobilienmarkt gibt, werden die Mietpreise von DLF vorgegeben und bezahlt. Der Inhaber von DLF gehört zu den 100 reichsten Leuten weltweit.

6) **Können Sie Ihre Antwort „Zielstrebigkeit“ als wichtigen Faktor für den Erfolg in Indien näher erläutern?**

Man muss genau wissen, was man in Indien will. Will man nur verkaufen oder auch Reparaturen und Instandsetzung mit anbieten. Dies muss klar definiert werden. Gerade weil Inder so schwammig sind, müssen sich Ausländer klar positionieren. Wenn man schwammig ist als Ausländer geht man unter. Bei der Positionierung und Definition der Unternehmenstätigkeit sind Beratungsunternehmen wichtig. Es funktioniert nicht, dass man sagt, ich fahr mal nach Indien und schau mal, was passiert.

7) **Inwiefern sind Steuern und Einfuhrbestimmungen aus Ihrer Sicht Markteintrittsbarrieren?**

Beides ist undurchsichtig und Regeln ändern sich stets. Diese häufigen Änderungen sind auch bedingt durch den Konflikt zwischen den beiden Hauptparteien, die BJP, die eher modern und fortgeschritten agiert und die eher konservative, nationalistische Partei. Dadurch kommt es häufig zu Reformen und man muss sich stets auf dem Laufenden halten.
Weiterhin sind die Zölle sind hoch.
Momentan wird gerade über ein Freihandelsabkommen zwischen der EU und Indien verhandelt, wobei es noch keine genauen Ergebnisse gibt.

8) **Können Sie bitte zu der gleichen Frage Ihre Antwort „nicht-tarifäre Handelshemmnisse, protektionistische Tendenzen“ erklären?**

Der Staat versucht das Land und die indischen Unternehmen zu schützen. Demzufolge sind Importzölle sehr hoch. Der Schutz und die Offenheit gegenüber ausländischen Unternehmen sind branchenabhängig und auch in den verschiedenen Bundesländern unterschiedlich. Oft wird mit einer großen Willkür gehandelt. Viele ausländische Unternehmen versuchen dies zu vermeiden, indem sie ein Joint Venture mit indischen Partnern eingehen. Damit genießen sie Schutz und der indische Partner kennt sich gut auf dem indischen Markt aus.

9) **Können Sie bitte Ihre Antwort betreffend der gesellschaftlichen Rahmenbedingungen und der daraus resultierenden Markteintrittsbarrieren näher erklären? Sie gaben als Antwort „interkulturelles Unverständnis, z.B. bezüglich der Handels- und Geschäftsmentalität" an.**

Viele Ausländer haben Schwierigkeiten die indische Mentalität zu verstehen, wobei Berater wichtig sind.
So bedeutet „Ja" oft „Nein" und „No problem" heißt oft, dass es ein Problem gibt. Häufig werden Versprechungen und Deadlines nicht eingehalten.

Danksagung und Verabschiedung.

Interview 2: Unternehmensberatung

- Datum: 25.01.2012, Uhrzeit: 16:24; Dauer: 44:38 min.
- Interviewpartner: Geschäftsführer
- Standort: München; Mumbai und Bangalore
- Unternehmensgröße: 15 Mitarbeiter davon vier in Indien; keine Angabe bezüglich des Jahresumsatzes

Da zuvor kein Fragebogen ausgefüllt wurde, folgt das Gespräch einem zuvor erarbeiteten Leitfaden, wobei sich der Interviewer an den Fragen aus dem erstellten Fragebogen orientierte.

Zuvor Begrüßung / Small-Talk...

1) **Was sind aus Ihrer Sicht wichtige Faktoren, um als ausländisches Unternehmen in Indien erfolgreich zu sein?**

Die zwei wichtigsten Dinge sind Kenntnisse des Marktes sowie Geduld. Dabei sollten Sie wissen, wie der Markt tickt und wie Sie Ihre Produkte auf dem Markt platzieren. So sind beispielsweise zunächst „Metro" und „VW" auf dem indischen

Markt gescheitert aufgrund fehlender Kenntnisse. VW hat den Polo vor 14 Jahren in Indien einführen wollen, wobei sie gescheitert sind. Der VW Polo war damals zu groß dimensioniert und nicht gefragt. Heutzutage werden auch große Autos angefragt, da die Mittelschicht wächst. Früher hingegen wurden nur sehr kleine Autos nachgefragt. Der VW Polo war unbekannt in Indien, hingegen war der VW Käfer sehr beliebt, jedoch wurde dieser nicht angeboten. Es ist wichtig den Markt zu kennen und zu wissen, wie die Geschmäcker sind. VW war als Marke für Busse bekannt, aber nicht für Autos. Mercedes hingegen ist sehr beliebt, allein schon wegen der Marke.
Ein weiteres Beispiel dafür, dass Kenntnisse des Marktes wichtig sind, kann ich Ihnen gern nennen: Im Jahr 2001 gründeten die Allianz AG und Bajaj Auto Ltd. das Joint Venture Bajaj Allianz Life Insurance Co. Ltd.. Obwohl seit einigen Jahren im Bereich Versicherungen eine 100-prozentige Direktinvestition möglich ist, hat die Allianz in den ersten fünf Jahren mit Bajaj zusammengearbeitet, um die Kenntnisse des indischen Partners für sich zu nutzen. Bajaj verkauft Mofas und hat vor allem junge Nachfrager im Portfolio. Die Kunden von Bajaj wurden vertrieblich von der Allianz genutzt und häufig als neue Kunden akquiriert.
Weiterhin sollten Sie erst eine Strategie vor Ort ausarbeiten und dann schnellst möglich umsetzen, da sich der Markt im stetigen Wandel befindet.

2) Wie sehen Sie die Verbreitung von Korruption?

Korruption ist in Indien ein weit verbreitetes Thema. In Deutschland gibt es compliances gegen Korruption, in Indien hingegen gibt es Berater für Korruption. So genannte PRO's, Public relation officers, kümmern sich um das Thema Korruption. Für einfache Genehmigung ist der finanzielle Aufwand gering. Umso mehr man bezahlt, umso schneller erledigen sich die Dinge. Oft sagt man, „Kein Geschäft ohne Korruption".
Kleine Menschen machen dies genauso wie große Unternehmen. Der Grund ist, dass viele Mitarbeiter miserabel bezahlt werden und sich etwas dazu verdienen müssen. Es gibt viele, die gegen Korruption sind, aber das Thema ist tief in den Köpfen der Inder und lässt sich nicht so einfach verdrängen. Einige Leute sind mittlerweile gierig geworden und machen richtig Geschäfte mit der Korruption, sie haben Luxusautos, Yachten und Bungalows oder ein Konto in der Schweiz mit mehreren Millionen drauf.

Es ist wichtig einen lokalen Experten zu haben, der sich auskennt und weiß, wen man wie viel bezahlen muss. Vor allem in größeren Unternehmen gibt es ganze Abteilungen, die sich diesem Thema widmen. In einem kleinen Unternehmen ist meist mindestens ein Mitarbeiter mit der Problematik Korruption beschäftigt.

3) **Wie schätzen Sie den Managementaufwand mit Behörden in Indien ein?**

Ich schätze den Aufwand genauso groß wie in Deutschland ein. Allerdings lässt sich in Deutschland vieles leichter delegieren, sodass sich das Management vom Aufwand befreien kann. In Indien muss der Geschäftsführer viele Dinge erledigen und kann diese nicht delegieren, somit ist es in Deutschland leichter.

4) **Was sind aus Ihrer Sicht Markteintrittsbarrieren aufgrund wirtschaftlicher Rahmenbedingungen wie hohe Bürokratie, fehlendes Beziehungsnetzwerk, fehlende Marktkenntnisse oder die hohe Konkurrenz?**

Dieses Thema hat sich in den letzten Jahren drastisch geändert. Heute ist die Umgebung wesentlich businessfreundlicher als vor 10 oder 20 Jahren. Der Preis für Dienstleistungen steigt zunehmend und alles wird professioneller. Es gibt für jegliche Dinge Dienstleister in Form von Beratern.

Das A & O ist ein gutes Beziehungsnetzwerk, sodass Partnerschaften sehr wichtig sind.

In Indien gibt es eine gestiegene Konkurrenz. Die führenden Handelspartner Indiens sind China und die USA, Deutschland hingegen ist auf Platz 17. 16 andere Länder waren schneller und sind somit Konkurrenten für die Deutschen.

Indien ist in den Bereichen IT, Textil, Mobilfunk und Logistik sehr professionell geworden. Jedoch ist die Bandbreite an die Dienstleistungen sehr gestiegen. So gibt es Angebote im Niedrig- aber auch im Hochpreissegment. Damit ist Indien sehr flexibel für Unternehmer. Für klein- und mittelständische Unternehmen empfehle ich lokale Berater, hingegen für große Unternehmen große Berater.

Wie schon gesagt, können fehlende Marktkenntnisse zu Markteintrittsbarrieren werden.

5) **Was sind aus Ihrer Sicht Markteintrittsbarrieren aufgrund gesetzlicher Rahmenbedingungen wie die Wahl der Unternehmensform, Steuern, Zölle oder Schutzrechte?**

Die Markteintrittsbarrieren in diesem Bereich sind meiner Meinung nach niedrig. Aufgrund des Beitrittes zur WTO sind die Zölle weitestgehend aufgehoben und vergleichbar mit den anderen Mitgliedsstaaten. Beispielsweise sind die Zölle für Agrarprodukte in Indien und Deutschland gleich hoch und liegen bei 20 Prozent. Olivenöl aus Italien ist doppelt so teuer wie in Indien, aufgrund der Einfuhrzölle. Autos werden in Indien kostengünstig produziert und dann in Deutschland verkauft. Die Verkaufspreise dürfen aufgrund deutscher Gesetze nicht unter der in Deutschland produzierten Autos liegen, sodass so Gewinne resultieren.

6) **Was sind aus Ihrer Sicht Markteintrittsbarrieren aufgrund gesellschaftlicher Rahmenbedingungen wie Religion, Kaste oder Wertigkeit der Familie?**

Hier gibt es eher operativ Probleme. Beispielsweise müssen Unternehmen überlegen, wo sie Produkte anbieten. In Gujarat gibt es ein Alkoholverbot, sodass hier keine Brauerei eröffnet und auch kein Alkohol verkauft werden sollte. In Goya hingegen trinken viele Leute Alkohol, sodass dies hier eher angeboten werden sollte. In Gujarat gibt es auch viele Vegetarier, sodass hier Fleisch nicht angeboten werden sollte. Man muss auf jedenfall die Regionen kennen.

Bei den letzten Volkszählungen gab es Überraschungen in puncto Religionszugehörigkeit. In Indien gibt es absteigend Hindus, Moslems, Christen und Buddhisten. Dabei ist die regionale Verbreitung durchwachsen und nicht mehr auf Regionen einzuordnen, sodass heraus Schwierigkeiten entstehen können. Aus Kasten hingegen resultieren keine Probleme.

Danksagung und Verabschiedung.

Interview 3: Automobilzulieferant

- Datum: 20.01.2012; Uhrzeit: 13:31; Dauer: 37:36 min.
- Interviewpartner: mittleres Management, männlich
- Standort: Dortmund; Chennai
- Unternehmensgröße: 140 Mitarbeiter weltweit davon 20 in Indien; circa eine Million Euro Jahresumsatz

Das Gespräch folgte einem Leitfaden, wobei einige spezielle Punkte des zuvor ausgefüllten Fragebogens detaillierter beleuchtet wurden.

Zuvor Begrüßung / Small-Talk...

1) **Warum entschied sich ihr Unternehmen für einen Markteintritt in Indien?**

Das war eigentlich kein Entschluss. Die Mutter namens Hinduja Gruppe hat einen Sitz in Indien und ist der Investor von uns. Die Hinduja Gruppe wollte, dass wirr einen Produktionsstandort in Indien hat, sodass sich eher die Frage stellte, wo in Indien ist der richtige Standort für uns. So ist der Bildungsstandard im Süden Indiens vergleichsweise hoch. Verschiedene Wirtschaftsbereiche sind in unterschiedlichen Regionen Indiens zu finden. Die IT ist beispielsweise in Bangalore angesiedelt. Ingenieure hingegen sind vor allem in Chennai zu finden, das auch als das „Detroit of India“ betitelt wird. So plant Daimler ab 2013 große Nutzfahrzeuge in Chennai zu bauen, BMW ist seit 2007 vor Ort und Hyundai hat auch eine Fabrikation in Chennai. Einer der größten Kunden von uns ist der Bushersteller Ashok Leyland, die ebenfalls in Chennai angesiedelt sind. Auf dieser Grundlage entschieden wir uns für den Standort Chennai. Chennai ist mittlerweile ein Cluster der Automobilbranche geworden, sodass immer mehr Zulieferer nach Chennai kommen. Außerdem gibt es viele Ingenieurschulen, sodass für Nachwuchs innerhalb der Region gesorgt wird. Bereits heutzutage ist der Zugang zu qualifizierten Mitarbeitern in Chennai recht einfach. Chennai ist eine Hafenstadt, sodass der Export nach Südostasien gut abgewickelt wird. Außerdem ist Thailand ein wichtiger Zulieferer, der von hieraus gut bedient werden kann.

2) Inwiefern sind aus Ihrer Sicht die Zusammenarbeit mit öffentlichen Verwaltungen und Behörden schlecht? Haben Sie dazu eventuell ein Beispiel?

Zum einen ist es schwierig Statistiken und Daten zu erhalten. In Deutschland ist dies viel einfacher aufgrund des Statistischen Bundesamtes. In Indien gibt es so etwas nicht, außerdem kann man sich auf Statistiken nur bedingt verlassen.
In Indien stellt sich die Frage, warum sollte eine indische Behörde jemanden in Deutschland helfen? Worin liegt der eigene Nutzen? Es ist immer am besten selbst vor Ort zu sein, wobei man viel Geduld benötigt und die Korruption weit verbreitet ist. Wenn man gute Kontakte vor Ort hat, läuft es wesentlich besser. Die Hinduja Gruppe löst so die Probleme von uns, wobei es besser ist, wenn wir nicht immer wissen, wie. Wir müssen unsere Unternehmensrichtlinien, compliances, befolgen und in Deutschland ist das Thema Korruption heikel beziehungsweise es ist verboten sich an ihr zu beteiligen. Wer sich erwischen lässt, hat seinen Ruf zu verlieren und muss mit gesetzlichen Konsequenzen rechnen. Im Prinzip ist es teurer, wenn man ständig nach Indien fliegt, um vor Ort alles zu regeln, als wenn man mal 100 Rupien bezahlt und so die Dinge beschleunigt.
Indische Unternehmen und auch Unternehmen aus Asien und Südafrika gehen mit dem Thema Korruption ganz anders um beziehungsweise haben sich darauf eingestellt. Dies ist für sie ein Wettbewerbsvorteil, da Genehmigungen schneller erfolgen und sie somit besser auf dem Markt agieren können.

3) Wie meinen Sie Ihre Aussage „Entwicklung zum Pull-Markt“ unter dem Punkt "Allgemein", betreffend der ersten Frage über wichtigsten Faktoren, um in Indien erfolgreich zu sein. Können Sie dies bitte näher erläutern?

Das Problem vieler Unternehmen in Deutschland ist, dass sie ein perfektes Produkt kreieren möchten und auch Garantiekosten möglichst gering halten möchten. In Indien ist dies anders. Die Unternehmen verkauften früher alles Mögliche ohne die Kundenwünsche zu analysieren beziehungsweise auf diese einzugehen, sodass Indien vor 15 Jahren noch ein Push-Markt war. Heutzutage entwickelt sich Indien zunehmend zu einem Pull-Markt. Der Grund dafür ist das die Mittelschicht wächst und mobiler wird. Der Primärsektor, also die Landwirtschaft, ist zwar weiterhin sehr

wichtig in Indien, aber die Nachfrage nach Dienstleistungen, also den Tertiärensektor, steigt. Die Verbraucher informieren sich vor dem Produktkauf, wobei häufig das Internet genutzt wird. Der Markt hat somit eine höhere Transparenz und die Verbraucher wollen keine aufgedrückten Produkte mehr. So werden Kundenanalysen und Lastenhefte zunehmend wichtiger.
Wichtig ist in Indien ein ausreichendes Produkt mit einer sehr guten Kostenstruktur herzustellen, da Indien ein low-cost-market ist. Die Funktionalität des Produktes steht im Vordergrund. Die Produkte müssen auf den Kunden ausgerichtet sein und es ist am besten vor Ort zu produzieren.

4) **Wie darf ich zu gleicher Frage die Antwort "Klare Trennung zwischen Arbeiter- und Managementlevel" verstehen?**

Auf der Arbeiterebene geht es hektisch zu, wobei alle etwas vorgeben zu wissen. Auf der Managementebene sollte man lieber alles klären, weil man dann den richtigen Ansprechpartner hat, der sich kümmert und in dessen Kompetenzbereich das Anliegen liegt.

5) **Können Sie bitte Ihre Antworten auf die Fragen betreffend der Markteintrittsbarrieren resultierend aus gesetzlichen und gesellschaftlichen Rahmenbedingungen näher erläutern? Als Markteintrittsbarrieren resultierend aus gesetzlichen Rahmenbedingungen kreuzten Sie die „Wahl der Unternehmensform“ sowie „Einfuhrbestimmungen / Zölle“ an und bei den Markteintrittsbarrieren resultierend aus gesellschaftlichen Rahmenbedingungen bestätigten Sie mit dem Ankreuzen, dass das Kastenwesen bedeutend für Sie sei. Können Sie dies bitte näher erläutern?**

Zu den gesetzlichen Rahmenbedingungen sind vor allem die Wahl der Unternehmensform sowie die Zölle für uns ausschlaggebend, sodass wir dies in Ihrem Fragebogen ankreuzten. Bezüglich der Wahl der Unternehmensform kann ich folgendes sagen: es gibt viele private limited's. Den genauen Vorteil weiß ich nicht, aber zumindest muss man nicht mit seinem Privatvermögen haften. Genaures kann ich Ihnen dazu leider nicht sagen, aber mir wurde berichtet, dass diese Form der Unternehmensform für ausländische Investoren am besten sei.

Betreffend der Zölle, kann ich Ihnen folgendes mitteilen: in Deutschland gibt es Warennummern, unter welche verschiedene Produkte laufen; in Indien werden die gleichen Produkte häufig in anderen Produktklassen eingeordnet, welches zur Folge hat, dass man stets andere Gebühren bei der Einfuhr bezahlen muss und dass ganze System sehr unübersichtlich ist.
Markteintrittsbarrieren, die aus gesellschaftlichen Rahmenbedingungen resultieren, sind unserer Meinung nach vielfach begründet aufgrund des Kastenwesens. Dieses wurde zwar 1947 offiziell abgeschafft, aber es wird auch heute noch gelebt. So bekommen Söhne aus hoher Kaste schneller einen Job oder einen Platz an einer angesehenen Universität. Beispielsweise bewarb sich der Sohn eines Priesters, der Brahmane war, um einen Studienplatz, als der Dekan wusste, um wem es sich handelt, hat der Sohn aus Angst vor Flüchen, die der Priester gegenüber dem Dekan aussprechen könnte, einen Platz an der Universität erhalten.

Danksagung und Verabschiedung.

Interview 4: Anlagen- und Maschinenbau

- Datum: 17.01.2012, Uhrzeit: 15:03, Dauer: 20:37 min.
- Interviewpartner: mittleres Management, männlich
- Standort: Wiesbaden; Pune
- Unternehmensgröße: 350 Mitarbeiter weltweit davon 25 in Indien; circa 30 Million Euro Jahresumsatz

Das Gespräch folgte einem Leitfaden, wobei einige spezielle Punkte des zuvor ausgefüllten Fragebogens detaillierter beleuchtet wurden.

Zuvor Begrüßung / Small-Talk...

1) **Warum haben Sie sich entschieden eine 100%-ige Tochtergesellschaft in Indien zu gründen?**

Dies war ein gemeinsamer Entschluss, da die Markterschließung zusammen mit einem anderen Unternehmen geplant war. Dieses Unternehmen ist jedoch ausgeschieden, sodass wir die Markterschließung dann allein vornahmen. Wir konzentrieren uns dabei auf unser Core-Business. Mit anderen Worten: Nachdem die Idee aufkam zusammen nach Indien zu gehen und diese gemeinsame Idee scheiterte, wollten wir das Potenzial Indiens nutzen und erschlossen den Markt mit unserem Kerngeschäft.

2) **Können Sie bitte Ihre Aussage bezüglich des Absatzmarktes „hohe Nachfrage auf dem Absatzmarkt, dennoch geringer Ertrag“ näher erläutern?**

In Indien sind die Margen sehr gering. Die Nachfrage ist zwar hoch, aber es gibt viele konkurrierende Firmen, ein Überangebot und eine starke Konkurrenz auf dem Markt. Daraufhin sinken die Preise. Die Kosten für den Support sind sehr hoch. Margen werden künftig immer niedriger.
In unserer Branche ist Qualität wichtig, jedoch ist auch hier die Preissensibilität hoch. Generell ist der Preis wichtiger als die Qualität. Man sollte zu günstigen Kosten produzieren und zu niedrigen Preisen verkaufen. Deshalb sollte man versuchen mit Zusatzleistungen die Margen zu steigern.

3) **Inwiefern schätzen Sie die Kooperation mit politischen Entscheidungsträgern und Banken als schlecht ein?**

Dies liegt vor allem an der hohen Bürokratie und der hohen Bestechlichkeit der Beamten.

4) **Inwiefern ist aus Ihrer Sicht die Umweltqualität in Indien schlecht?**

Dies begründe ich mit den folgenden Schlagwörtern: Lärm, Dreck und enorme Hitze. Viele produzierende Unternehmen in Indien achten nicht auf die Umwelt. Vor allem in den Bereich der Müllverbrennung wird die Umwelt nicht geschont. Oftmals werden Abwässer in Flüsse geleitet.

5) **Wie darf ich Ihre Antwort „Kostenstruktur“ zu der Frage bezüglich der Besonderheiten klein- und mittelständischer Unternehmen im Vergleich zu großen Unternehmen beim Markteintritt in Indien verstehen? Können Sie dies bitte näher erläutern?**

Die Markteintrittsbarrieren für klein- und mittelständische Unternehmen sind höher und ein Kostenvorteil entsteht, wenn man sich nicht auf mehrere Produkte gleichzeitig konzentriert, sondern sukzessive den Markt bearbeitet. Die allgemeinen Kosten sind in Indien sehr hoch. In größeren Unternehmen wird die Vielzahl an Mitarbeitern, die nicht zur Leistungserbringung des Unternehmens dienen wie Sekretärin, Buchhalter, Teejunge und so weiter, leichter aufgefangen als in kleinen Unternehmen, da die Allgemeinkosten auf mehrere produktive Mitarbeiter umgeschlüsselt wird.

6) **Inwiefern sehen Sie die gesetzlichen Rahmenbedingungen Steuern und Einfuhrbestimmungen sowie Zölle als Markteintrittsbarrieren an? Bitte begründen Sie dies kurz.**

Die Steuern in Indien sind hoch und das System ist unübersichtlich. Es gibt ständig neue Auslegungsmöglichkeiten, sodass man sich stets auf dem Neuesten halten muss. Hinzu kommt die hohe Bürokratie. Generell werden einheimische Unternehmen bevorzugt. So werden absichtlich unterschiedliche Steuern erhoben, um Markteintrittsbarrieren für ausländische Unternehmen künstlich zu schaffen.

7) **Inwiefern sehen Sie „die Qualifikation und Einsatz der Mitarbeiter“ als interkulturelle Herausforderung an? Bitte begründen Sie dies kurz.**

Es ist schwierig Mitarbeiter zu motivieren. Dies liegt an den Kasten und der fehlenden Verbindlichkeit. Inder nehmen das Leben so hin, wie es ist. Das Ausbildungsniveau ist niedrig und die Inder müssen erst praktisch ausgebildet werden. Dabei fehlt ihnen häufig der Eigenantrieb.

Danksagung und Verabschiedung.

Interview 5: Unternehmensberatung

- Datum: 17.01.2012, Uhrzeit: 14:32; Dauer: 20:17 min.
- Interviewpartner: Geschäftsführerin
- Standort: Hamburg
- Unternehmensgröße: 10 Mitarbeiter weltweit davon keine in Indien; keine Angabe bezüglich des Jahresumsatzes

Das Gespräch folgte einem Leitfaden, wobei einige spezielle Punkte des zuvor ausgefüllten Fragebogens detaillierter beleuchtet wurden.

Zuvor Begrüßung / Small-Talk...

1) **Inwiefern schätzen Sie das Ausbildungsniveau der Inder schlecht ein? Können Sie dies kurz begründen?**

Wir haben das Feedback vieler Unternehmen bekommen, dass das Ausbildungsniveau in Indien schlecht ist. Topqualifizierte Arbeitnehmer wurden im Ausland ausgebildet und sind oft sehr teuer, vergleichbar mit den Kosten, die wir in Deutschland für gute Arbeitskräfte bezahlen. Der „normale" Inder, auch wenn er von der Hochschule kommt, hat nur theoretisches Wissen und benötigt eine mehrmonatige Ausbildung um sich praktische Fähigkeiten anzueignen und um in einem Unternehmen eingesetzt werden zu können.
Weniger förderlich ist auch, dass das Lehrmaterial in den Universitäten oft veraltet ist und es keine duale Ausbildung gibt.

2) **Inwiefern sehen Sie die gesetzlichen Rahmenbedingungen Steuern und Einfuhrbestimmungen sowie Zölle als Markteintrittsbarrieren an? Bitte begründen Sie dies kurz.**

Das Thema Steuern ist unübersichtlich und die Steuern sind sehr hoch. Das Ganze ist ein komplexes Thema, da je nach Bundesstaat unterschiedliche Steuersätze anfallen und somit die Steuern je nach Bundesstaat unterschiedlich hoch sind.

Die Zölle wurden in den letzten Jahren, vor allem nach der Marktöffnung Indiens beziehungsweise Indiens Liberalisierung zwar drastisch gesenkt, für manche Produkte sind sie aber immer noch zu hoch und es gibt Zusatzabgaben, wie die Education Cess. Für eingeführte Waren sind die Steuern im internationalen Vergleich sehr hoch und liegen bei 26 bis 30 Prozent. Beispielsweise sollten Automobilhersteller in Indien Autos bauen, da die Einfuhr zu teuer ist, so erging es beispielsweise BMW.

3) **Wie darf ich Ihre Aussage betreffend Korruption und „speed money“ verstehen? Können Sie dies bitte erläutern?**

„Speed money“ wird in vielen Bereichen gefordert, damit Prozesse wie Genehmigungen schneller von statten gehen. Es ist vom jeweiligen Unternehmen und ihren Policies abhängig, ob sie sich auf die Zahlung von „speed money“ einlassen. Manche Unternehmen sprechen sich direkt dagegen aus und wollen damit nichts zu tun haben. Oft wird die Zahlung von „speed money“ nicht als Korruption, sondern als Aufpreis für Dienstleistungen angesehen, quasi als eine Gefallensleistung, damit es schneller geht. Wer nicht zahlt, muss länger warten. Bei der Beantragung von Visumsanträgen geht es höchstbürokratisch zu und oft wird „speed money“ erforderlich.

4) **Unter dem Abschnitt „Allgemein“ nennen Sie als einen wichtigen Faktor um in Indien erfolgreich zu sein „die Auswahl des richtigen Personals“. Ich stelle es mir aufgrund der Vielzahl an potenziellen Arbeitskräften schwierig vor das richtige Personal zu finden. Haben Sie Tipps für Unternehmer, die genau vor dieser Herausforderung stehen?**

Die Personalauswahl sollte mit einem lokalen Berater vor Ort gemeinsam geschehen. Als Deutscher allein ist dies sehr schwierig, weil man die Inder oft schlecht einschätzen kann. Auf eine Anzeigenschaltung melden sich hunderte Bewerber und es ist schwierig als Unerfahrener die Selektion durchzuführen. Viele der Bewerber verschönern beispielsweise ihren Lebenslauf und ein lokaler Berater sieht dies sofort und weiß, wer am besten in das Unternehmen passt. Der lokale Berater sollte für die Auslese der Bewerbungen zuständig sein sowie

Bewerbungsgespräche führen, da sie sich auf dem indischen Markt am besten auskennen und zwischen den Zeilen lesen beziehungsweise hören können.
So lässt sich oft anhand des Namens und des Ausbildungsweges auf die Kaste schließen. Auf die Kastenzugehörigkeit sollte man vor allem bei der Besetzung von Führungspositionen achten, da einige Inder aus einer höheren Kasten sich nicht gern von jemand aus einer niedrigeren Kaste führen lassen möchten. Dienstleister unterstützen gern bei der Personalsuche und sind hilfreich. Auch die AHK unterstützt Unternehmen bei der Personalsuche.

5) **Haben Sie Empfehlungen für klein- und mittelständische Unternehmen für den Markteintritt in Indien oder weitere Anmerkungen, die für mich wichtig sein könnten?**

In Indien herrscht eine stark ausgeprägte Preissensibilität, das heißt Inder legen Wert auf preiswerte Produkte, wobei die Qualität nicht so wichtig ist. Für Unternehmen bedeutet dies, dass sie sich oft durch niedrige Preise von der Konkurrenz abheben möchten. Dadurch entstehen niedrige Gewinnmargen. Im asiatischen Raum sind die Gewinnmargen in Indien mit am geringsten.

Außerdem sollten bereits etablierte Produkte auf den indischen Markt angepasst werden, da sonst lokale Abnehmer nicht angesprochen werden und das Unternehmen Absatzprobleme bekommt. Beispielsweise werden Kühlschränke mit Schlössern davor produziert, da die Bediensteten im Haus sich nicht unerlaubt am Kühlschrank bedienen sollen. Ein weiteres Beispiel kann ich auch aus der Automobilbranche nennen. Da Inder selbst nicht fahren, sondern einen Fahrer dafür haben, ist die Innenausstattung entsprechend den indischen Gegebenheiten anzupassen. So ist der vordere Bereich des Wagens spärlich eingerichtet, hingegen ist die Rückbank gut ausgestattet, beispielsweise ist oft am Rücksitz ein Fernseher montiert, damit der Gefahrene Unterhaltung hat.

Danksagung und Verabschiedung.

Interview 6: Nahrungsmittelindustrie

- Datum: 16.01.2012; Uhrzeit: 17:16 Uhr; Dauer: 27:46 min
- Interviewpartner: mittleres Management; männlich
- Standort: Hamburg; Pune
- Unternehmensgröße: 500 Mitarbeiter weltweit davon 5 in Indien; keine Angabe bezüglich des Jahresumsatzes

Das Gespräch folgte einem Leitfaden, wobei einige spezielle Punkte des zuvor ausgefüllten Fragebogens detaillierter beleuchtet wurden.

Zuvor Begrüßung / Small-Talk...

1) **Können Sie bitte kurz begründen, inwiefern Sie die Arbeitsmoral in Indien als sehr gut einschätzen?**

Die Arbeitsmoral ist in Indien sicherlich unterschiedlich, aber hier in Pune sind wir sehr zufrieden. Wie ich gehört habe, ist dies vielerorts anders. Hier bei uns bleibt keiner aus familiären Gründen weg oder kommt später. Wir sind wirklich sehr zufrieden.

2) **Inwiefern sind aus Ihrer Sicht die Zusammenarbeit mit öffentlichen Verwaltungen und Behörden sowie Banken schlecht? Haben Sie dazu eventuell ein Beispiel?**

Grund hierfür ist vor allem die lange Bearbeitungszeit, die benötigt wird und aufgrund der hohen Bürokratie immens ist. Wir haben zum Beispiel einen Geldbetrag von unserem Büro in Hongkong auf unser Konto in Indien erhalten und wollten dies am Jahresende wieder zurück überweisen. Der ganze Prozess hat 18 oder 20 Tage gedauert und ging durch verschiedene Banken. Wir mussten mehrere Formulare ausfüllen und jedes Mal Geld bezahlen, sodass die eigentliche Überweisung recht teuer für uns wurde. Normalerweise kann man das Ganze per Online-Banking innerhalb kurzer Zeit abwickeln, aber in Indien war das nicht möglich.

Auch die Zusammenarbeit mit politischen Entscheidungsträgern ist schlecht, aufgrund der hohen Bürokratie.

3) **Inwiefern schätzen Sie den Managementaufwand in Indien als besonders hoch ein?**

In Indien müssen jegliche Kleinigkeiten vom Chef entschieden werden, sodass viel mehr Zeit für Dinge aufgewendet wird, die in Deutschland von anderen mitgetragen oder übernommen werden.

4) **Bitte begründen Sie Ihre Aussage, dass die Verfügbarkeit der Elektrizitätsversorgung in Indien schlecht ist.**

Wir sind mit vielen Stromausfällen konfrontiert, sodass wir Generatoren einsetzen müssen, welches zu weiteren Kosten führt und sehr aufwendig ist. Ansonsten würden unsere Systeme unterbrochen werden. Um Datenverluste zu vermeiden, haben wir ein Back-up-System für unsere Technik eingerichtet, welches wiederum mit Kosten verbunden war und ist.

5) **Können Sie bitte kurz begründen, warum Sie die Qualität von Räumen als schlecht einschätzen?**

Wir haben einen Neubau gekauft, der gerade mal vier Jahre alt war und dessen Qualität auf den ersten Blick als gut erschien. Mit der Zeit erkannten wir, dass der Aufwand die Räume in Schuss zu bringen höher ist, als erwartet war. Nach Reparaturarbeiten von indischen Unternehmen mussten wir zusätzliche Arbeiten erbringen, da die Qualität der Reparaturen nicht ausreichend war. Die Qualität von bereits genutzten Räumen ist sehr schlecht, da die Inder mit Dingen, die ihnen nicht gehören, schlecht umgehen. Aufgrund dessen kann ich nur die Anmietung oder den Kauf von wirklich neuen Räumen oder Gebäuden empfehlen. Auch wenn diese anfangs teurer erscheinen, sind die Reparaturkosten für bereits gebrauchte Immobilien so hoch, dass die Kosten und der Aufwand für neue Immobilien sprechen.

6) **Inwiefern sind Sie mit den allgemeinen Betriebskosten unzufrieden?**

Indien ist relativ teuer, wenn man bedenkt, dass die Qualität, die man für sein Geld bekommt, unterdurchschnittlich ist und Nachbesserungen sehr oft erforderlich sind. Deshalb wird alles teuer, auch wenn es anfangs als preiswert erscheint. Wie ich bereits sagte, fällt ständig der Strom aus, sodass wir mithilfe von Generatoren dieses Problem beseitigten, welches aber zu erhöhtem Aufwand und zusätzlichen Kosten führte.

7) **Können Sie bitte Ihre Unzufriedenheit in Bezug auf die Kosten für Miete und Grundstückspreise kurz begründen?**

Die Kosten für Miete und Grundstückspreise sind recht teuer und die Qualität ist eher schlecht, vor allem in großen Ballungsräumen. So kann ein schäbiger Raum 1.000,- Euro kosten und eine unverzinste Kaution von 14 oder 15 Prozent fällig werden.

8) **Inwiefern sind Sie mit den Kosten für Abgaben und Steuern unzufrieden?**

Das ganze System ist sehr unübersichtlich und es gibt eine Vielzahl an Steuern. Sie fragen zum Beispiel vier Leute zum Thema Service Tax und erhalten fünf verschiedene Antworten. Außerdem ist der Export aufgrund von Steuern sehr teuer.

9) **Können Sie bitte Ihre Antworten unter dem Gebiet "Allgemein", zweite Frage: „Überzeugungsentscheidung“ näher erläutern?**

Unser Inhaber hat beobachtet, wie sich die Märkte entwickeln und sich entschieden nach Indien zu gehen. Diese Entscheidung wurde von ihm die ganze Zeit getragen und richtigerweise betrachtete er den Markteintritt in Indien als Chefsache.
Ich möchte noch hinzufügen, dass klein- und mittelständische Unternehmen es oft leichter haben als große multinationale Unternehmen, da sie oft hochspezialisiert sind und so den Markt besser bearbeiten können. Große Unternehmen müssen häufig mit der Politik zusammenarbeiten und sind damit gebundener. Außerdem verfolgt die Politik manchmal andere Ziele als man selbst.

Außerdem möchte ich noch erwähnen, dass eine gewisse Unternehmensgröße und vor allem Ausdauer notwendig sind, um nicht kaputt gemacht zu werden.

10) Können Sie bitte Ihre Antwort „Wertigkeit der Familie“ auf die Frage betreffend der Markteintrittsbarrieren resultierend aus gesellschaftlichen Rahmenbedingungen näher erläutern?

Die Wertigkeit der Familie kann zu einem Problem werden, muss sie aber nicht. Oftmals wird die Entscheidung über künftige Mitarbeiter von der Familie getroffen, da die Familie am besten weiß, wo das Familienmitglied arbeiten sollte. Hierbei werden vor allem Großunternehmen bevorzugt, da diese einen guten Ruf haben und für die soziale sowie medizinische Versorgung der Mitarbeiten sorgen.
Die Familie in Indien ist auch in Bezug auf die Religion beziehungsweise religiöse Feiertage sehr wichtig. Vor allem religiöse Feiertage sind in Indien besonders wichtig und Arbeitgeber sollten diese genau kennen und den Arbeitsnehmern freigeben, da diese Tage mit der Familie verbracht werden. Andernfalls können die Mitarbeiter verärgert sein und von der Arbeit fortbleiben.

11) Haben Sie Empfehlungen für klein- und mittelständische Unternehmen für den Markteintritt in Indien oder weitere Anmerkungen, die für mich wichtig sein könnten?

Wichtig ist, dass man den Markteintritt und die weiteren Geschäfte in Indien aus Überzeugung und Interesse macht und nicht nebenbei versucht diesen großen Markt zu bedienen. Das geht schief. Inder sind viel emotionaler und man muss versuchen die Leute für sich zu gewinnen, um in Indien erfolgreich zu sein. Außerdem müssen die Mitarbeiter viel an die Hand genommen und geführt werden, welches wiederum aufwendig ist.
Einige Unternehmen scheitern, weil sie die Kosten falsch betrachten. So ist die Ausbildung der Inder oft schlechter als in Deutschland, sodass mehr Arbeitskräfte benötigt werden, was zu erhöhten Kosten führt. Sehr gut ausgebildete Mitarbeiter sind in Indien sehr teuer und absolut kein Grund nach Indien zu gehen.
Abschließend möchte ich sagen, dass man nach Indien gehen sollte, weil man davon überzeugt ist und nicht weil man Kosten sparen will.

Danksagung und Verabschiedung.

Interview 7: Anlagen- und Maschinenbau

- Datum: 12.01.2012, Uhrzeit: 19:08, Dauer: 20:34 min.
- Interviewpartner: Geschäftsführer
- Standort: Weitefeld
- Unternehmensgröße: 120 Mitarbeiter weltweit davon keine in Indien, sondern Lizenzvertrag mit Tata Motors ltd.; circa 30 Millionen Euro Jahresumsatz

Das Gespräch folgte einem Leitfaden, wobei einige spezielle Punkte des zuvor ausgefüllten Fragebogens detaillierter beleuchtet wurden.

Zuvor Begrüßung / Small-Talk...

1) **Wie darf ich mir die Zusammenarbeit mit Tata Motors vorstellen und wieso haben Sie sich für diese mit Tata Motors entschieden?**

Die Unternehmensphilosophie von Tata Motors hat uns gefallen und passt gut mit unser eigenen Philosophie zusammen. Deshalb entschieden wir uns, dass Tata Motors unser Lizenzpartner wird. Wir haben somit keine eigenen Mitarbeiter vor Ort, sondern nur einen freien Mitarbeiter, der bei Tata Motors in Delhi und Mumbai für uns nach dem Rechten schaut.
Wir lassen Tankcontainern in Lucknow herstellen und sind in Zukunft offen für eine Kooperation mit Tata Motors, wobei wir eine Minderheitsbeteiligung anstreben.

2) **Wie schätzen Sie den indischen Absatzmarkt ein?**

Auf dem indischen Markt ist der Mengenverkauf unserer Produkte eine strategische Investition und wir sehen den indischen Markt als wichtigen Zukunftsmarkt. Momentan bezahlen wir auf den Lizenzvertrag drauf und es lohnt sich bis dato noch nicht. In Indien sollte man keine kurzfristigen finanziellen Interessen haben. Wir werden schätzungsweise in den nächsten drei Jahren in den roten Zahlen sein und es geht langsam bergauf. Der Charme Indiens ist die Masse und die Perspektive.

3) **Wie schätzen Sie die Zusammenarbeit mit den öffentlichen Behörden ein?**

Die indischen öffentlichen Behörden sind mit den europäischen Strukturen nicht vergleichbar. In Indien sind Netzwerke sehr wichtig. Außerdem ist die Verbreitung von Korruption hoch und für Nicht-Inder ist es sehr schwierig mit den öffentlichen Behörden zusammenzuarbeiten.

4) **Wie schätzen Sie die Zusammenarbeit mit finanziellen Infrastruktur-einrichtungen ein?**

Bei der Zusammenarbeit mit finanziellen Infrastruktureinrichtungen muss man viel Geduld und gute deutsche Bankpartner haben, um seine Geschäfte abwickeln zu können. Dabei kann der Geldtransfer teilweise monatelang dauern. In Indien wird nicht verstanden, warum Deutsche bei Geschäften Druck machen, da Inder ein anderes Zeitverständnis haben und der Zeitbegriff gedehnt ist.

5) **Können Sie bitte Ihre Aussage „Preissensibilität" zu den wichtigsten Faktoren, die von entscheidender Bedeutung sind, um in Indien erfolgreich sind, näher erklären?**

Das Spektrum zwischen arm und reich ist sehr hoch, wobei die Produktpreise den indischen Verhältnissen angepasst werden sollten. In Indien ist ein geringer Preis wichtiger als die Qualität der Produkte und das Verkaufsargument. Wenn Sie teurer verkaufen als ihre Konkurrenz, haben Sie schlechte Chancen. Die Inder schauen nämlich zunächst auf den Preis bevor sie sich näher mit dem Produkt befassen. Deshalb ist es wichtig kostengünstig zu produzieren und das Produkt entsprechend preiswert zu verkaufen.

Danksagung und Verabschiedung.

Interview 8: Unternehmensberatung

- Datum: 07.01.2012, Uhrzeit: 15:00, Dauer: 46:12 min.
- Interviewpartner: Geschäftsführer
- Standort: Chemnitz
- Unternehmensgröße: 6 Mitarbeiter, davon keine in Indien; keine Angabe bezüglich des Jahresumsatzes

Da zuvor kein Fragebogen ausgefüllt wurde, folgt das Gespräch einem zuvor erarbeiteten Leitfaden, wobei sich der Interviewer an den Fragen aus dem erstellten Fragebogen orientierte.

Zuvor Begrüßung / Small-Talk...

1) **Laut Ihrer Internetseite sind Sie vor allem Unternehmensberater mit dem Schwerpunkt der arabischen Länder? Wie sind Sie zu Indien gekommen?**

Das ist richtig. Seit 1993 bin ich im Bereich der Firmeninvestitionen tätig. Seit 1997 berate ich Unternehmen bezüglich Investitionen und Beratung in Tschechien. Im Jahre 1999 kamen die arabischen Länder hinzu und darauf habe ich mich spezialisiert. Seit einigen Jahren berate ich nun auch Unternehmen, die einen Markteintritt in Indien planen. Ich bin vor allem auf den Unternehmen aus den Branchen des Maschinenbaus und KFZ-Baus in Indien spezialisiert. Wir unterstützen klein- und mittelständische Unternehmen, ab 250 beziehungsweise 300 Mitarbeitern. Dabei beraten wir von Deutschland aus, führen Analysen durch und schlagen Korrespondenzpartner vor.

2) **Welche Faktoren sind aus Ihrer Sicht wichtig, um in Indien erfolgreich zu sein?**

Zunächst einmal dauert der Markteintritt in Indien lange, sodass vor allem Geduld und Ausdauer sehr wichtig sind. Meiner Meinung nach, sind 200 bis 500 Mitarbeiter ideal für den Markteintritt in Indien, da man so flexibler ist und über die entsprechenden Ressourcen verfügt.

Um in Indien erfolgreich zu sein, sollte man sich interkulturell auf seine Geschäftspartner einlassen und nicht versuchen den deutschen Stil durchzusetzen. Dabei hilft es ein Joint Venture mit einem indischen Partner zu gründen, da man dann von den Beziehungen des indischen Partners profitiert und so sein Netzwerk erweitern beziehungsweise ergänzen kann. Ohne Fachleute beziehungsweise Beratern dauert es 3 bis 4 Jahre bis man erfolgreich in Indien ist. Der Einsatz von Berater ist gerade beim Mittelstand wichtig, wobei der Eintritt circa 2 bis 3 Jahre dauert.

Es ist außerdem wichtig, den Markteintritt in Indien gut vorzubereiten, gerade in Hinblick auf die Finanzen und das richtige Personal. Die Vorbereitungen für den Markteintritt dauern 1 bis 3 Jahre. Weiterhin sollte man gute Landeskenntnisse und Kenntnisse über die Leute haben.

3) **Wie schätzen Sie die Zusammenarbeit mit den indischen Behörden ein?**

Beim Management mit Behörden stößt man auf eine große Bürokratie und ich empfehle Partner vor Ort, da ein gutes Beziehungsnetzwerk wichtig ist. Gerade in Bezug auf die indischen Behörden ist das Thema Freundschaftsleistung in Form von Korruption ausschlaggebend und viele Deutsche sehen dies als negativ an und scheuen deshalb den Markteintritt.

4) **Haben Sie weitere Tipps für deutsche klein- und mittelständische Unternehmen in Bezug auf deren Markteintritt in Indien?**

Der Bund unterstützt klein- und mittelständische Unternehmen. Programme, bei den 5.000 bis 6.000 EUR gefördert werden, sterben aus und es werden eher größere Projekte gefördert. Wichtig für die Projekte sind gute Projektmanager.

Danksagung und Verabschiedung.

Interview 9: Software-Unternehmen

- Datum: 06.01.2012, Uhrzeit: 16:27 Uhr, Dauer: 25:47 min.
- Interviewpartner: Geschäftsführer
- Standort: Stuttgart; Hyderbad
- Unternehmensgröße: 16 Mitarbeiter, davon 12 in Indien; keine Angabe bezüglich des Jahresumsatzes

Da zuvor kein Fragebogen ausgefüllt wurde, folgt das Gespräch einem zuvor erarbeiteten Leitfaden, wobei sich der Interviewer an den Fragen aus dem erstellten Fragebogen orientierte.

Zuvor Begrüßung / Small-Talk...

1) **Welche Faktoren sind aus Ihrer Sicht wichtig, um in Indien erfolgreich zu sein?**

Hierbei sind vor allem Landeskenntnisse und Kenntnisse der Geschäftskultur wichtig. Indien ist ein großes Land mit unterschiedlichen Kulturen, Unterschieden zwischen Nord und Süd, unterschiedlichen Sprachen und bestimmte Bundesländer haben unterschiedliche Geschäftskulturen. All diese Unterschiede und Besonderheiten sollte man kennen, wenn sich an einem bestimmten Standort in Indien niederlässt, um in Indien erfolgreich aktiv zu sein. Hierbei ist die Wahl des Standortes wichtig, wobei für den Erfolg es ausschlaggebend ist, die jeweilige regionale Geschäftskultur und die richtigen Leute vor Ort zu kennen. Außerdem sind reale Erfahrungen wichtig und man sollte Berater vor Ort sowie ein großes und vor allem gutes Beziehungsnetzwerk haben.

2) **Wie schätzen Sie die Zusammenarbeit mit den indischen Behörden ein?**

Wenn man sich gut auskennt und weiß, wer der richtige Ansprechpartner ist, gibt es bei der Zusammenarbeit mit indischen Behörden keine Probleme. Es sind zwar nicht die gleichen Verhältnisse wie in Deutschland, wo alles relativ automatisch funktioniert. Aber wie gesagt, in Indien muss man die richtigen Leute kennen oder

Berater beziehungsweise Partner vor Ort haben, die sich gut auskennen und das richtige Verständnis für Behörden haben, und dann funktioniert das Ganze.

3) Worin sehen Sie Markteintrittsbarrieren für deutsche klein- und mittelständische Unternehmen in Indien?

Als hohe Barrieren sind die Kultur und für Deutsche die anglosächische Gesetzgebung zu sehen. So werden Vertragsabschlüsse nicht so gehandhabt wie in Deutschland, sodass Verträge weitaus länger sind und alles Eventualitäten enthalten sein müssen.

Kulturell kann ich sagen, dass die Kasten keine wichtige Rolle im Geschäftsleben spielen, wie man vielleicht meinen könnte. Größere Barrieren hingegen liegen begründet in den vielen unterschiedlichen Sprachen sowie den Unterschieden zwischen Nord und Süd. Obwohl Indien eine Nation ist, findet man hier viele verschiedene Sprachen und Kulturen, die zu berücksichtigen sind.

Früher war das Thema der unterschiedlichen Zeitwahrnehmung zwischen Europäern und Indern ein ständiges Problem. Mittlerweile ist die Zeitwahrnehmung der Inder fast so wie das, der Europäer. Die Inder haben erkannt, dass sie sich den Kunden anpassen müssen, vor allem in der IT-Branche.

Weiterhin ist jedoch das Verständnis von Qualität in Deutschland und Indien unterschiedlich. Inder haben nicht dieses hohe Qualitätsbewusstsein und müssen dies von den Deutschen lernen. Auch die Technik ist in Deutschland viel fortgeschrittener. Beispielsweise sind die Züge in Indien heutzutage auf den Stand wie in Deutschland zu der Nachkriegszeit. Entsprechend kennen sich die meisten Inder mit der modernen Technik nicht so gut aus und man muss es ihnen beibringen, da sie aber sehr lernfähig sind, geht dies recht schnell.

Eine Markteintrittsbarriere, die für alle deutschen Investoren zutrifft, ist das einheimische Unternehmen mehr durch den Staat geschützt werden. Wie zum Beispiel durch Zölle für ausländische Waren. Ein Beispiel dafür ist, dass BMW beispielsweise keine Autos importieren darf, sondern nur die Teile und vor Ort produzieren muss. Meist unterliegen Dienstleistungsunternehmen geringeren Kontrollen.

Zu dieser Frage abschließend möchte ich sagen, dass viel Vorbereitung und Informationen über das Land wichtig sind.

4) Welchen Besonderheiten beziehungsweise Herausforderungen stehen klein- und mittelständische Unternehmen beim Markteintritt in Indien gegenüber, im Vergleich zu großen Unternehmen?

Zum einen verfügen klein- und mittelständische Unternehmen über weniger Ressourcen und zum anderen sind sie risikofreudiger. Außerdem haben Großunternehmen oftmals die Möglichkeit sich besser auf den Markteintritt vorzubereiten und können aufgrund ihrer Ressourcen leichter Marktforschungen, Delegationsreisen und so weiter durchführen. Generell haben klein- und mittelständische Unternehmen weniger Zeit sich vorzubereiten und investieren schneller. Vergleichsweise, informieren sich mehr Großunternehmen vor Ort, und klein- und mittelständische Unternehmen eher aus Deutschland heraus, meist über Generalkonsulate, Botschaften und der AHK.

Danksagung und Verabschiedung.

Interview 10: Unternehmensberatung

- Datum: 06.01.2012, Uhrzeit: 13:06; Dauer: 36:54 min
- Interviewpartner: Geschäftsführer
- Standort: Berlin; Pune
- Unternehmensgröße: 15 Mitarbeiter, davon 4 in Indien; circa eine Millionen Euro Jahresumsatz

Das Gespräch folgte einem Leitfaden, wobei einige spezielle Punkte des zuvor ausgefüllten Fragebogens detaillierter beleuchtet wurden.

Zuvor Begrüßung / Small-Talk...

1) Welche Unternehmensform empfehlen Sie deutschen Investoren in Indien als Unternehmensberater?

Ich empfehle gerade klein- und mittelständischen Unternehmen die Gründung einer 100%-igen Tochtergesellschaft und keiner Vertretung, da Tochtergesellschaften einfach zu gründen sind. Die Gründung einer Tochtergesellschaft kann man schnell im Internet machen und benötigt nur 100.000 indische Rupien, sodass die Kosten und der Aufwand vergleichsweise gering sind.

Hingegen kann es größere Schwierigkeiten bei der Zusammenarbeit mit finanziellen Infrastruktureinrichtungen geben, so zum Beispiel bei der Kontoeröffnung. Weiterhin kann die Erlangung der Director Identification Number schwierig sein, die für die Gründung einer Gesellschaft in Indien notwendig ist. Bei der Kontoeröffnung und Erlangung der Director Identification Number muss der Wohnsitz zum Beispiel mithilfe von Telefonrechnungen, welche die Adresse enthält, nachgewiesen werden. So wird festgestellt, ob der ausländische Investor einen festen Wohnsitz im Ausland hat.

Für klein- und mittelständische Unternehmen empfehle ich, dass sie eine private limited gründen, da dies einfach ist und den Anforderungen genügt. Bei großen Konzernen muss die Unternehmenswahl gründlicher überdacht werden. Dies soll aber nicht das heutige Thema sein.

2) Gibt es besondere Vorteile für klein- und mittelständische Unternehmen in Indien zu investieren?

Ich sehe keine Vorteile, aber auch keine Nachteile, die sich auf die Größe des Unternehmens zurückführen lassen. Der Brandname von größeren Unternehmen kann vorteilhaft sein wegen des guten Rufes. Regional kann aber auch ein kleines Unternehmen nach gewisser Zeit besser gestellt sein als größere Unternehmen, wenn sie zu guter Qualität produzieren. Vorteilhaft für kleine Unternehmen kann die Steuererleichterung sein, wenn sie einen geringen Jahresumsatz haben. Hierbei liegt die Grenze bei 10 Lakh, welches circa 15.000 Euro entspricht.

3) Worin sehen Sie Schwierigkeiten beziehungsweise Herausforderungen besonders für deutsche klein- und mittelständische Unternehmen bei dem Markteintritt in Indien?

Viele Unternehmen, gerade klein- und mittelständische Unternehmen, unterschätzen die benötigte Zeit für den Markteintritt und den Aufbau des Unternehmens in Indien. Es dauert eine gewisse Zeit bis das Geschäft profitabel ist, sodass ein langer Atem und Ausdauer eine wesentliche Voraussetzung für den Erfolg in Indien sind.

Ein häufiges Problem sind die interkulturellen Missverständnisse. So wollen Deutsche alles schnell erledigen. Inder hingegen sind entspannter und legen viel Wert auf Beziehungen. Dabei sollte man nicht vergessen, dass Beziehungen eine gewisse Zeit benötigen und nicht von heute auf morgen entstehen. Meiner Meinung nach sind fünf Jahre für den Aufbau von Beziehungen gar nichts und sollten auf jedenfall eingeplant werden.

Eine weitere Herausforderung für ausländische Unternehmen ist die Korruption, die in Indien als hoch betrachtet wird. Transaktionskosten sind umso geringer, umso mehr Leute man kennt und umso besser die Beziehungen sind. Weiterhin haben deutsche Geschäftsbanken Schwierigkeiten Rupien nach Indien zu transferieren, sodass Korrespondenzbanken eingesetzt werden und Gebühren anfallen. Andersherum, also Euro nach Indien zu überweisen ist hingegen kein Problem.

Zum Schluss, darf ich Ihnen nach einen Tipp für Ihre Bachelorarbeit geben? Ich denke, dass es gut wäre, wenn Sie am Ende der Arbeit etwas über die Handelskammern schreiben. Vielleicht hinterfragen Sie, wie deren Unterstützung aussieht und ob sie wirklich hilfreich sind. Beispielsweise ist die AHK überteuert. Für einen Antrag für eine Unternehmensgründung mit allem drum und dran nimmt die AHK 6.000 Euro, kleine Berater nehmen hingegen meist nur 3.000 Euro. Bei der Zusammenarbeit mit der AHK sind Beziehungen wichtig, da man so leichter Unterstützung erhält. Wenn die AHK ein Projekt für interessant empfindet, unterstützt sie dies, ansonsten muss man allem hinterher rennen. Ich empfehle Ihnen weiterhin sich mit dem GIRT auseinanderzusetzen. Dies ist der German-Indian Round Table, ein Verein von Kaufleuten und Industrieller, die sich alle zwei Monate treffen.

Danksagung und Verabschiedung.

Interview 11: Metallverarbeitende Industrie

- Datum: 04.01.2012; Uhrzeit: 10:08; Dauer: 43:41 min.
- Interviewpartner: Geschäftsführerin
- Standort: Aue; Indore
- Unternehmensgröße: 220 Mitarbeiter, davon 35 in Indien; circa 60 Millionen Euro Jahresumsatz

Da zuvor kein Fragebogen ausgefüllt wurde, folgt das Gespräch einem zuvor erarbeiteten Leitfaden, wobei sich der Interviewer an den Fragen aus dem erstellten Fragebogen orientierte.

Zuvor Begrüßung / Small-Talk…

1) **Zunächst interessiert mich, warum Sie laut Ihrer Angabe auf dem Fragebogen nicht erneut in Indien investieren möchten? Sie schreiben, dass Sie gut in Indien gestartet haben und es dann aber nicht dabei geblieben ist, dass Sie als Freunde behandelt wurden. Können Sie dies bitte näher erläutern?**

Um diese Frage zu beantworten muss ich ein wenig ausholen. Das Joint Venture läuft seit fünf Jahren und wir haben komplett neu gebaut. Das heißt wir haben das Gelände gekauft, die Firma gebaut und alles komplett ausgestattet. Wir gründeten unser Unternehmen zusammen mit zwei weiteren Partnern: einen französischen und einen indischen.

Dabei hat sich die Zusammenarbeit im Laufe der Zeit eher verschlechtert als verbessert. Inder sind Menschen, die brauchen zuallererst persönliche Beziehungen. Das heißt, das läuft alles auf Freundschaften hinaus. Die anfängliche freundschaftliche Beziehung hat sich dann aber permanent verschlechtert. Es gab Differenzen über Aufgabenstellungen des Geschäftsführers hier und wie Dinge abgewickelt werden und wie sie nicht abgewickelt werden. Es sind auch nie Vereinbarungen eingehalten worden zu Terminen, wann Monats-Reportings da zu sein haben. Wir haben permanent nachgefragt und die Inder unter Druck gesetzt: Wir haben gesagt, wenn eine Woche bevor wir losfliegen die Unterlagen nicht da

sind, werden wir nicht losfliegen. Und dann hat es geklappt, aber auch mit Verzögerungen.
Dann nehmen die es eben auch mit der Betriebswirtschaft nicht so genau. Die haben dann halt Dinge anders gerundet. – Also in der Buchhaltung da muss ja alles stimmen. Da gibt's kein plus / minus irgendwas. In der Buchhaltung muss es stimmen bis auf den letzten Cent und wenn der nicht da ist, dann muss er gesucht werden. Das hat uns manchmal nächtelang beschäftigt.

Jedenfalls sind wir im letzten Jahr zum Laufen gekommen, also in 2011. Aber davor mussten wir immer wieder Geld reinschießen, weil die den Umsatz nie gebracht haben, den sie versprochen hatten. Und ich hatte an sich vor, die Firma in die schwarze Zahl zu bringen, jetzt, also in 2011. Soweit sind wir ja nun fast auch gekommen. Aber... Bei uns ist dann halt etwas dazwischen gekommen. Wir haben seit 30.06. einen neuen Mehrheitsaktionär. Und der Gesellschaftsvertrag hat da eine Klausel drin, die bei einem „Change of Control" in Kraft treten kann. Bei Änderungen in der Aktionärsstruktur dürfen die anderen Parteien kündigen. Leider haben die Inder dann Anfang Oktober und auch die Franzosen eine Kündigung an uns geschickt. Ohne überhaupt mit uns darüber zu sprechen und für mich ist das ein dermaßen Vertrauensbruch gewesen...Man MUSS ja nicht kündigen, man KANN! Da ist dann alles nur über Anwälte gelaufen. Wir haben der Kündigung dann zugestimmt, Anfang Dezember oder Mitte Dezember, weil es sowieso kein Vertrauensverhältnis mehr gibt.

2) Welche Faktoren sind aus Ihrer Sicht wichtig, um in Indien erfolgreich zu sein?

Ganz wichtig ist die Zeit. Wir hätten viel mehr Zeit gebraucht. Da Sie sich ja auf den Mittelstand konzentriert haben, ist das eben ein anderes Thema, als wenn man in einem Großkonzern ist. Die dann praktisch ihre Mitarbeiter, die sie ins Ausland schicken, ein ganzes oder ein halbes Jahr schulen, auf bestimmte Dinge, kulturelle Sachen und dann auch Zeit haben. – Wir haben keine Zeit. Das ist also das größte Problem für den Mittelstand so ein Projekt anzugehen, so ein riesiges, dass man das eigentlich nebenbei macht. Die Firma hier ist auch mit fast 200 Mitarbeitern besetzt und dann das da drüben noch... Und dann ist man an sich prinzipiell unter Druck. Die Woche, die man dann drüben ist... Zeitverschiebung kommt noch dazu... Und die Inder die haben es dann wirklich drauf alle Probleme, die wirklich maßgebend sind, bringen sie dann innerhalb von zwei Stunden bevor man nach Hause muss und da müsste man dann wirklich die Zeit haben und sagen: Jetzt bleibe ich. Dann kommt aber auch alles andere wieder durcheinander... Also Zeit ist eins der maßgeblichen Probleme oder besser gesagt, Dinge, die man haben muss, wenn man so etwas angeht. Mehr Zeit!

Weiterhin sind ausreichen finanzielle Ressourcen notwendig, weil da wird immer wieder Geld gebraucht wird, immer wieder! Ungeplant! Das heißt, wir mussten immer wieder nachschießen, ungeregelt, unkontrolliert. Dann musste ein Tempel gebaut werden, das hat natürlich auch Geld gekostet. Da haben sie uns erklärt: „Ohne Tempel geht ja gar nicht! Die Firma braucht einen Tempel." Okay, gut.

Außerdem wäre ein Rechtsanwalt oder Berater in unserem Fall wirklich gut gewesen.

3) Wie schätzen Sie die Lebensbedingungen in Indien ein?

Vor fünf Jahren war es auch noch mal wesentlich schlechter, als es heute dort ist. Das hat sich in den fünf Jahren jetzt doch sehr positiv entwickelt, das ganze Land. Es hört langsam auf, dass Millionen Menschen auf der Straße oder an den Straßenrändern leben. Es sind immer noch die Slums da, aber es hat sich wesentlich verbessert: Es wurde der Flughafen gebaut, das war alles ein altes krautiges Zeug da in Delhi, es war eine Katastrophe. Aber das ist jetzt ein moderner Flughafen wie alle anderen in der Welt auch. Es wird auch die Obdachlosigkeit weggehalten, das haben wir vor fünf Jahren alles nicht gehabt. Da standen Menschenmassen draußen. Wenn man rausgekommen ist, wurde einem fast versucht die Tasche wegzureißen.

Also, je südlicher, desto besser wird es dann, unten an der Küste vor allen Dingen. Das ist dann ganz anders und es gibt auch Städte, die sind sehr europäisch geprägt. Aber gerade in Mumbai fliegt man ganz dicht über die Häuser und Slums hinweg. In Indore, wo wir waren, sage ich immer, es sieht aus wie im Mittelalter. Viel Schlamm und Dreck und keine Häuser wie in mittelalterlichen Filmen.

Es ist ja kein einfaches Arbeiten in Indien: Die Riesenhitze, die Zeitverschiebung ist eben ungünstig. Wenn man nur kurz da ist, ist die ungünstig – nach Osten immer. Erst mal, um im Osten sofort arbeiten zu können am nächsten Tag, dann ist das ungünstig. So, und unter diesen Bedingungen – Essen, Wasser, was alles da kommt und Krankheiten und und und...

Und diese komplizierte Englisch, das haben Sie ja bestimmt auch mitbekommen. Ich meine, im Smalltalk geht das alles noch, aber die sprechen ja ein komplizierteres Englisch als die Amerikaner. Das ist einfach auch schwer. Und dann diese ganzen verschiedenen Vertragsinhalte... - Angelsächsisches Recht... Man hätte sich normalerweise, bevor man sowas anfängt, komplett weiterbilden müssen. Hier rausnehmen, ein halbes oder dreiviertel Jahr das angelsächsische Recht zumindest ansatzweise mal – ich sage mal: „...ein bisschen studieren" – und das indische auch... Und dann kann man etwas anfangen.

In Indien hätte man vielleicht besser einen deutschen CEO einstellen sollen, aber der müsste dann wirklich gut gebildet sein. Das müsste wirklich einer sein, der sich mit den Gesetzen auskennt, die da drüben herrschen. Ansonsten wird der untergebuttert.

Danksagung und Verabschiedung.

Interview 12: Rechts- und Steuerberatung

- Datum: 07.12.2011, Uhrzeit: 10:02; Dauer: 39:12 min.
- Interviewpartner: Geschäftsführerin
- Standort: München
- Unternehmensgröße: 2 Mitarbeiter davon keine in Indien; keine Angabe bezüglich des Jahresumsatzes

Da zuvor kein Fragebogen ausgefüllt wurde, folgt das Gespräch einem zuvor erarbeiteten Leitfaden, wobei sich der Interviewer an den Fragen aus dem erstellten Fragebogen orientierte.

Zuvor Begrüßung / Small-Talk...

1) **Nennen Sie bitte die vier wichtigsten Aspekte um in Indien erfolgreich zu sein.**

Zunächst sollte man Marktstudien führen und sich viel Zeit lassen sowie man darf sich nicht reinreden lassen.
Wenn man mit Partner zusammenarbeitet, sollte man sich mehrere Partner anschauen und aus diesen eine Auswahl treffen. Bei der Zusammenarbeit mit lokalen Partnern ist es wichtig Anreize zu schaffen, einen persönlichen Kontakt zu haben, sie stets zu kontrollieren und diese eng zu führen.
Ganz wichtig ist auch ein besonderes Augenmerk auf Verträge zu legen, da diese kompliziert sind und viele Details enthalten. Man selbst sollte jegliche Details in den Verträgen festhalten, um spätere Auseinandersetzungen zu vermeiden.
Für die Entwicklung eines Unternehmens ist es wichtig sich von klein auf groß zu entwickeln, das heißt, wenn ein Produkt in Indien erfolgreich ist, kann man weitere Produkte entwickeln und vermarkten und so weiter. Man sollte erst schauen, ob ein Produkt in Indien erfolgreich ist, um festzustellen, welche Produkte in Indien gefragt sind.
Außerdem ist es wichtig, dass das deutsche Topmanagement das Indiengeschäft stets begleitet und dahinter steht.

2) **Wie schätzen Sie das Ausbildungsniveau und die Qualifikation der Arbeitskräfte in Indien ein?**

Viele Inder, die frisch von der Universität kommen, müssen zunächst praktisch ausgebildet werden, da ihnen die praktische Erfahrung fehlt. Das Problem für klein- und mittelständische Unternehmen ist die Kontrolle der Qualität der Zulieferer sowie das Ausbildungsniveau der Arbeiter, die bei Zulieferern arbeiten. Größere Unternehmen können dies besser kontrollieren.
Gerade in den Clustern Delhi, Pune, Gujarat, Chennai, Hyberbad, Kalkutta und Bangalore steigt das Gehalt. In diesen Clustern ist das Gehaltsniveau hoch, aber auch die Qualifikation der Arbeitskräfte ist hier am besten. In diesen Clustern müssen die Arbeitskräfte durch zusätzliche Erfolgskomponenten sowie Zusatzleistungen wie Fortbildungen, Autos, Handys, Versicherungen gebunden werden, damit die Fluktuation sinkt.

3) Wie schätzen Sie die Nachfrage auf dem Binnenmarkt ein?

Indien ist kein Markt, sondern besteht aus vielen regionalen Märkten. Die Märkte sollten auf Cluster herunter gebrochen werden und man sollte sich nicht auf verschiedene Kaufkräfte konzentrieren, sondern sich auf eine Gruppe spezialisieren. Marktkenntnisse sind in Indien sehr wichtig. Die Binnennachfrage ist in Indien höher als in China. Dementsprechend sollten Unternehmen ihr Augenmerk darauf legen und ihre Produkte in Indien verkaufen, statt diese zu exportieren. Dies trifft vor allem auf Industrie- und Konsumgüter zu, die in Indien auch die höchste Nachfrage genießen. Noch hat die Landwirtschaft in Indien einen hohen Anteil, dennoch steigt die Nachfrage zunehmend nach Dienstleistungen, die 60 Prozent des BIP's ausmachen.

4) Wie schätzen Sie Kooperationen mit anderen Unternehmen ein?

Wenn man ein Joint Venture gründet, ist es wichtig sich Zeit für Verhandlungen zu nehmen. Früher konnte ein Partner eines Joint Ventures nicht mit einem anderen Partner in der gleichen Branche zusammenarbeiten ohne das Einverständnis des anderen Joint Venture Partners. Dies war vertraglich geregelt. Generell ist es wichtig in Verträgen alles bis ins Detail festzuhalten, da das indische Recht auf dem britischen Gesetz aufbaut und somit Case Law angewandt wird. Dies ist sehr aufwendig und Gerichtsverfahren dauern bis zu zehn Jahre.

5) Wie schätzen Sie die infrastrukturellen Gegebenheiten in Indien ein?

Der innerörtliche Nahverkehr ist sehr schlecht in Bezug auf Qualität.
Bezüglich der Elektrizitätsversorgung sind Backup-Systeme notwendig, gerade für IT-Unternehmen.
Flächen, Bauland, Gebäude und Räume werden stets neu gebaut, aber meist auch zunehmend teurer, gerade in Mumbai. Oft sind diese schmutzig und dunkel.

6) Wie schätzen Sie die Lebensbedingungen in Indien ein?

Die Verfügbarkeit von Wohnungen und Häusern ist relativ schlecht, gerade wenn man nach etwas preiswerten sucht. Vor allem in Vierteln, in denen viele Europäer

wohnen, ist es teuer, da zum Standard internationale Schulen, Gärtner und Fahrer gehören. In Unternehmen kommen zum normalen Personal weitere Mitarbeiter wie Copyboys, Teaboys und Empfangsdame, die in die Lohnbuchhaltung mit einfließen und die betreut werden müssen, sodass der Aufwand steigt.
Weiterhin ist zu sagen, dass viele Europäer Probleme mit den klimatischen Bedingungen in Indien haben.

7) **Haben Sie Empfehlungen für klein- und mittelständische Unternehmen für den Markteintritt in Indien oder weitere Anmerkungen, die für mich wichtig sein könnten?**

Die Position des Generalmanagers sollte mit Indern bekleidet werden. Häufig sind lokale Manager in Indien tätig, da diese sich am besten auf dem indischen Markt auskennen.
Von vielen Unternehmen, die nach Indien gegangen sind, habe ich positives Feedback bezüglich ihrer Aktivitäten in Indien gehört. So haben sie schneller als gedacht beziehungsweise schneller als ihnen vorher prophezeit wurde die Gewinnschwelle erreicht. Die Vielzahl der Unternehmen ist mit ihrer Entscheidung zufrieden nach Indien gegangen zu sein.

Danksagung und Verabschiedung.

Interview 13: Unternehmensberatung

- Datum: 06.12.2011, Uhrzeit: 09:15 Uhr, Dauer: 01:30 h
- Interviewpartner: Geschäftsführer
- Standort: München; New Delhi
- Unternehmensgröße: 10 Mitarbeiter davon vier in Indien; keine Angabe bezüglich des Jahresumsatzes

Da zuvor kein Fragebogen ausgefüllt wurde, folgt das Gespräch einem zuvor erarbeiteten Leitfaden, wobei sich der Interviewer an den Fragen aus dem erstellten Fragebogen orientierte.

Zuvor Begrüßung / Small-Talk...

1) **Welche Faktoren sind aus Ihrer Sicht wichtig, um in Indien erfolgreich zu sein?**

Zunächst sollte beachtet werden, dass Indien kein Land, sondern ein Subkontinent ist. Jedes Bundesland hat seine eigene Sprache und Kultur. Deshalb sollten sich Unternehmen auf eine Region beschränken und nicht versuchen ganz Indien mit seinen Produkten oder Dienstleistungen zu bedienen. Schon die Engländer verließen 1947 Indien, weil sie mit der indischen Kultur nicht klar kamen. Ihre Schwierigkeit war die fehlende Anpassungsfähigkeit. Und das ist der wichtigste Faktor um in Indien erfolgreich zu sein: Anpassungsfähigkeit. Investoren sollten nicht versuchen die Inder zu ändern, sondern sich auf die indische Kultur einlassen und versuchen diese zu verstehen. Unterstützung erhalten kleinere Unternehmen zum Beispiel vom German Center in New Delhi. Diese haben festgestellt, dass viele Deutschen oftmals unter sich bleiben und somit sich nicht mit der indischen Kultur beschäftigen, sodass sie Schwierigkeiten haben die indische Kultur zu verstehen. Hingegen stellen sich viele Inder auf Deutsche ein. Viele junge Inder wollen Deutsch lernen und erlernen dies häufig in den Goethe Instituten. Sie arbeiten dann häufig in Call Centern. Aber nicht alle Inder kommen mit den Neuerungen klar, die aufgrund der Reformen das Land vorangebracht haben. Erschreckend ist die hohe Anzahl von Selbstmorden in Indien. So gab es 300.000 Selbstmorde innerhalb von 3 Jahren von Indern, die mit den Neuerungen nicht klar kamen.

Aber auch der Aufbau von Netzwerken ist sehr wichtig, da in Indien vieles über Kontakte läuft und vieles einfacher macht.

Außerdem ist es wichtig, dass Deutsche keine Vorurteile haben sollten. Denn aufgrund der Größe des Landes ist kein Inder mit einem anderen vergleichbar. Was auf den einen zustimmt, muss auf den anderen gar nicht passen.

Weiterhin sollten Deutsche positiv denken, um in Indien erfolgreich zu sein.

Wichtig ist, dass Deutsche Interesse am anderen zeigen. Dabei ist das Thema Familie besonders wichtig, da Inder sehr familiär sind und die Familie in ihrem Mittelpunkt steht.

2) Wie schätzen Sie das Wirtschaftsklima in Indien ein?

Das Wirtschaftsklima in Indien ist aus meiner Sicht gut. Angeblich kann man in Indien gute Geschäfte machen, weil Englisch von jedem gesprochen und verstanden wird. Es ist richtig, dass die Amtsprache Englisch ist und Akten auf Englisch geführt werden. Dennoch macht man die besten Geschäfte, wenn man die jeweilige regionale Sprache beherrscht und die jeweilige Geschäftskultur versteht. Wenn man dies berücksichtigt, steht einem erfolgreich Markteintritt in Indien nicht im Wege.

3) Wie schätzen Sie den Managementaufwand in Indien ein?

Der Managementaufwand ist in Deutschland genauso hoch wie in Indien, wenn man als Ausländer in Deutschland investieren möchte. In Deutschland müssen ausländische Investoren viele Formulare ausfüllen, wenn sie in Deutschland ein Unternehmen gründen. Genauso ist es auch in Indien.

4) Welchen Besonderheiten beziehungsweise Herausforderungen stehen klein- und mittelständische Unternehmen beim Markteintritt in Indien gegenüber?

Deutsche erleben oft einen Kulturschock und verstehen die indische Kultur nicht. So erging es auch Frau Merkel. Sie wollte in Indien einen Tempel besuchen, die man, wie viele wissen, barfuss betritt, sie trug Badelatschen und wurde skeptisch betrachtet.

Vielen Deutschen fehlen die soft skills, um mit Menschen anderer Kulturen umgehen zu können. Sie haben auf der anderen Seite aber den Ruf, dass sie gute Technik besitzen und gute Produkte herstellen. Generell sind deutsche Unternehmen gut Indien angesehen und sie sind dafür bekannt, dass sie für die medizinische Versorgung ihrer Mitarbeiter sorgen. Gewisse Eigenheiten sollten Deutsche jedoch beibehalten. So wie ihre Pünktlichkeit. Denn Inder wissen, dass

Deutsche pünktlich sind und haben sich darauf eingestellt. Deshalb sollten Deutsche auch in Indien pünktlich sein.
Besonders in Indien, im Vergleich zu Deutschland ist auch, dass Frauen sind in der Berufswelt mehr respektiert werden und häufiger auf der Managementebene vertreten sind.
Indern ist Fairness für gute Geschäfte wichtig und es werden meist win-win-Situationen angestrebt.
Interessant ist vielleicht noch, dass Indien der größte ausländische Investor in Ostdeutschland ist.

Danksagung und Verabschiedung.

Interview 14: Industrie- und Handelskammer

- Datum: 24.11.2011, Uhrzeit: 11:24 Uhr; Dauer: 15:49 min.
- Interviewpartner: Mitarbeiterin
- Standort: München
- Unternehmensgröße: keine Angaben bezüglich der Mitarbeiteranzahl und des Jahresumsatzes

Da zuvor kein Fragebogen ausgefüllt wurde, folgt das Gespräch einem zuvor erarbeiteten Leitfaden, wobei sich der Interviewer an den Fragen aus dem erstellten Fragebogen orientierte.

Zuvor Begrüßung / Small-Talk...

1) **Worin sehen Sie Schwierigkeiten beziehungsweise Herausforderungen besonders für deutsche klein- und mittelständische Unternehmen bei dem Markteintritt in Indien?**

Die Frage kann ich Ihnen nur allgemeingültig für deutsche Unternehmen beantworten, wobei meine Antworten wohl auch oder gerade für klein- und mittelständische Unternehmen zutreffen. Da ich nur kurz Zeit habe, werde ich Ihre Frage nur kurz beantworten können.

Zunächst sind die kulturellen Unterschiede zu nennen. So werden Zusagen missverstanden bzw. nach Vertragsabschluss nachverhandelt. Zudem sind die Vertragsverhandlungen generell langwierig.

Auch durch die hohe Bürokratie dauert in Indien alles länger, was durch die stark verbreitete Korruption verstärkt wird.

Glücklicherweise wurde in diesem Jahr (2011) die gängige Praxis abgeschafft, nach der ein Partner aus einem Joint Venture nur mit der Zustimmung des anderen Geschäftspartners herauskommt, gerade wenn er in der gleichen Branche erneut tätig sein möchte. Früher sind viele Investoren daran gescheitert, sodass zunehmend weniger Joint Ventures in Indien gegründet wurden.

Es gibt eine hohe Anzahl an Hochschulabsolventen und einfachen Mitarbeitern wie teaboys, aber es ist schwierig Facharbeiter, die Maschinen bedienen können, zu finden. Zudem weisen die Universitätsabschlüsse hohe Unterschiede auf, sodass ein Ingenieur nicht gleich Ingenieur ist und man sich mit den verschiedenen Hochschulen auseinandersetzen muss.

Des Weiteren sollten die Produkte preislich an Indien angepasst werden und brauchen nicht overengineered sein. Sie müssen vielmehr an die indischen Besonderheiten angepasst werden, damit sie alltagstauglich sind. So sind teure Küchengeräte meist überflüssig, da sie vom Haushaltspersonal bedient werden, die sich meist nur mit einfachen Geräten auskennen. Weiterhin muss der vordere Bereich eines Autos nicht gut ausgestattet sein, da die meisten Inder chauffiert werden. Aufgrund dessen ist der Ausbau des hinteren Bereichs weitaus wichtiger.

Die vielen Stromausfälle in Indien machen den Einsatz von Generatoren notwendig.

Danksagung und Verabschiedung.

Bibliography

Agarwal, M. (2009): India's Economic Future: Education, Technology, Energy and Environment, New York / Oxford, 2009.

Bain, J. S. (1956): Barriers to New Competition: Their Character and Consequences in Manufacturing Industries, New Jersey, 1956.

Berekoven, L. / Eckert, W. / Ellenrieder, P. (2009): Marktforschung. Methodische Grundlagen und praktische Anwendung, 12th edition, Wiesbaden, 2009.

Berndt, R. / Fantapié Altobelli, C. / Sander, M. (2010): Internationales Marketing-Management, 4th edition, Berlin, 2010.

Bütler, C. (2010): Internationale Unternehmensführung: Entscheidungsorientierte Einführung, Munich, 2010.

Chacko, E. (2007): From brain drain to brain gain: reverse migration to Bangalore and Hyderabad, India's globalizing high tech cities, in: Geo Journal 2007, 68, p. 131 – 140.

Chopin, C. (2009): Logistikstrategien für Indien, Norderstedt, 2009.

Das, A. K. / Mohanty, P. K. (2007): Human Rights In India, New Delhi, 2007.

Das, K. (2007): SMEs in India: Issues and possibilities in times of globalization, Bangkok, 2007.

Davis, H. J. D. / Chatterjee, S. R. / Heuer, M. (2006): Management in India: trends and transition, New Delhi, 2006.

Dülfer, E. (1999): International Management in Divers Cultural Areas, Munich, 1999.

Eschlbeck, D. (2006): Internationale Wirtschaft: Rahmenbedingung, Akteure, räumliche Prozesse, Munich, 2006.

Flick, U. (1995): Qualitative Forschung - Theorie, Methoden, Anwendung in Psychologie und Sozialwissenschaften, Hamburg, 1995.

Flick, U. / Kardorff, E. / Steinke, I. (2007): Qualitative Forschung - Ein Handbuch, 5th edition, Hamburg, 2007.

Freiling, J. / Reckenfelderbäumer, M. (2010): Markt und Unternehmung: Eine marktorientierte Einführung in die Betriebswirtschaftslehre, 3rd edition, Wiesbaden, 2010.

Germany Trade and Invest (2010): Praxisleitfaden Indien, Bonn, 2010.

Hitt, M. A. / Ireland, D. / Hoskisson, R. E. (2010): Strategic Management: Competitiveness & Globalization, 9th edition, Hamshire, 2010.

Höhner, B. (2007): Der Markteintritt in China. Die Internationalisierung kleinerer und mittlerer Unternehmen, Hamburg, 2007.

Holtbrugge, D. / Friedmann, C. B. (2011): Geschäftserfolg in Indien: Strategien für den vielfältigsten Markt der Welt, Heidelberg, 2011.

Hüttner, M. / Schwarting, U. (2002): Grundzüge der Marktforschung, 7th edition, Munich, 2002.

Ihlau, O. (2008): Weltmacht Indien. Die neue Herausforderung des Westens, Munich, 2008.

Indira Gandhi National Open University (2006): Unit 11: Market structure and barriers to entry, New Delhi, 2006.

Kirch, S. (2003): Marktstrategien für deutsche Produkte in Indien, Diss., Würzburg, 2003.

Lamnek, S. (2005): Qualitative Sozialforschung – Lehrbuch, 4th edition, Weinheim, Basel, 2005.

Mayer, H. O. (2008): Interview und schriftliche Befragung. Entwicklung, Durchführung, Auswertung, 4th edition, Munich, 2008.

McAuley, A. (2001): International Marketing: Consuming Globally, Thinking Locally, Chichester, 2001.

Mehl-Lammens, P. (2006): Geschäftserfolg Indien. Der Business-Guide für den indischen Subkontinent, Zurich, 2006.

Mitterer, K. / Mimler, R. / Thomas, A. (2006): Beruflich in Indien. Trainingsprogramm für Manager, Fach- und Führungskräfte, Göttingen, 2006.

Müller, O. (2006): Wirtschaftsmacht Indien: Chance und Herausforderung für uns, Munich, 2006.

OECD (2011): OECD – Wissenschafts-, Technologie- und Industrieausblick 2010, Indien, Paris, 2011.

Ossola-Haring, C. / Ruh, W. (2008): Wachstumsmarkt Indien. Das Investitionshandbuch für Unternehmen und deren Berater, Munich, 2008.

Pepels, W. (2012): Handbuch des Marketing, 6th edition, Munich, 2012.

Pilny, K. (2006): Tanz der Riesen: Indien und China prägen die Welt, Frankfurt, 2006.

Reiger, H. / Haas, B. (2010): Quantitative Sozialforschung. Eine Einführung, Vienna, 2010.

Rodewald, A. (2007): Business Know-how in Indien. So wird Ihre Geschäftsreise zum Erfolg, Heidelberg, 2007.

Saini, D. S. (2011): Employment law framework: structure and potential hurdles, in: Budhwar, P. S. / Varma, A. (eds): Doing Business in India: Building Research-based Practice, Oxford, 2011, p. 43.

Schaffer, R. / Agusti, F. / Earle, B. (2009): International Business Law and Its Environment, 7th edition, Mason, 2009.

Schumann, S. (2011): Repräsentative Umfrage, Praxisorientierte Einführung in empirische Methoden und statistische Analyseverfahren, 5th edition, Munich, 2011.

Tandler, A. (2011): Indiens ganz alltäglicher Terror, in: Die Welt, Issued on: 15.07.2011.

Todd, P. R. / Javalgi, R. G. (2007): Internationalization of SMEs in India. Fostering entrepreneurship by leveraging information technology, 2nd edition, Bingley, 2007.

Waldkirch, K. (2006): Geschäftserfolge in Indien. Erfolgsfaktoren erkennen, Perspektiven entwickeln, Märkte erschließen, Wiesbaden, 2006.

Wamser, J. (2005): Standort Indien. Der Subkontinentalstaat als Markt und Investitionsziel ausländischer Unternehmen, Diss., Münster, 2005.

Weidlich, T. / Yates, A. / Dietz, P. (2011): Ausländische Geschäftsaktivitäten in Indien, Cologne, 2011.

Wildemann, H. / Engelmeier, T. (2011): Markteintrittsbarrieren in den indischen Energiemarkt, Munich, 2011.

Wiskot, G. (2009): Götter, Handys und Geschäfte. Wirtschaftsstandort Indien, Karlsruhe, 2009.

Zotz, V. (2006): Die neue Wirtschaftsmacht am Ganges. Strategien für langfristigen Erfolg in Indien, Heidelberg, 2006.

Web-references

DE International (2011): Marktprofil Indien. URL: http://www.chemnitz.ihk24.de/2011/linkableblob/486076/.3./data/indien_1-data.pdf (07.06.2012)

Embassy of India (2012): Indo-German Bilateral Relations. URL: http://www.indianembassy.de/indo_german_relation.php (30.05.2012)

European Commission (2005): Europa – Enterprise – The new SME definition – User guide and model declaration. URL: http://ec.europa.eu/enterprise/policies/sme/files/sme_definition/sme_user_guide_en.pdf (11.05.2012)

European Commission (2011): Trade and Investment Barriers Report 2011. Engaging our strategic economic partners on improved market access: Priorities for action on breaking down barriers to trade. URL: http://trade.ec.europa.eu/doclib/docs/2011/march/tradoc_147629.pdf (19.07.2012)

Federal Offices (2009): Anteile kleiner und mittlerer Unternehmen an ausgewählten Merkmalen 2009. URL: https://www.destatis.de/DE/ZahlenFakten/GesamtwirtschaftUmwelt/UnternehmenHandwerk/KleineMittlereUnternehmenMittelstand/Tabellen/SonstigeDienstleistungen.html (14.05.2012)

Federal Offices (2011): Länderprofil. G-20 Industrie- und Schwellenländer. Indien. URL: https://www.destatis.de/DE/Publikationen/Thematisch/Internationales/Laenderprofile/Indien.pdf?__blob=publicationFile (31.05.2012)

Germany Trade & Invest (2011): Wirtschaftstrends Indien. Jahreswechsel 2011 / 2012. URL: https://www.gtai.de/GTAI/Content/DE/Trade/Fachdaten/PUB/2011/12/pub201112058008_16593.pdf (23.06.2012)

Germany Trade & Invest (2012): Wirtschaftsdaten kompakt: Indien. URL: http://www.gtai.de/GTAI/Content/DE/Trade/Fachdaten/MKT/2008/07/mkt200807555613_159630.pdf (30.05.2012)

Gorawantschy, B. / Suermann, F. (2010): Konfliktherd Kaschmir: Neue Wege zum Dialog? URL: http://www.kas.de/wf/doc/kas_20620-1522-1-30.pdf?100928104629 (19.10.2012)

Handelskammer Hamburg (2010): International. Indien – Länderbericht. URL: http://www.hk24.de/international/laenderinformationen/asien/362082/indien.html;jsessionid=FD4621BE757E84BB129BFA3794912B22.repl22 (31.05.2012)

IfB Bonn (2011): KMU Definition des IfM Bonn. URL: http://www.ifm-bonn.org/index.php?id=89 (14.05.2012)

IHK Würzburg-Schweinfurt (2011): Merkblatt. Zollbestimmungen – Indien. URL: http://www.wuerzburg.ihk.de/fileadmin/user_upload/pdf/International/LAENDERBERICHTE/Indien/Zoll.pdf (20.07.2012)

Indo-German Chamber of Commerce (2011): Annual Review 2011: German Investments in India. URL: http://indien.ahk.de/fileadmin/ahk_indien/Bilder/2012_news_and_info/ger_inv_in_india.pdf (20.10.2012)

Ministry of Commerce & Industry (2008): Press Note 7 (2008) - Consolidated Policy on Foreign Direct Investment. URL: http://pib.nic.in/newsite/erelease.aspx?relid=39600 (19.10.2012)

OECD (2007a): Competition and Barriers to Entry. URL: http://www.oecd.org/dataoecd/9/59/37921908.pdf (10.05.2012)

OECD (2007b): Economic Survey of India, 2007. URL: http://www.oecd.org/dataoecd/17/52/39452196.pdf (07.06.2012)

The Heritage Foundation (2012): India, 2012. URL: http://www.heritage.org/index/pdf/2012/countries/india.pdf (15.07.2012)

Transparency International Deutschland e.V. (2010): Corruption Perception Index 2011. URL:
http://www.transparency.de/Tabellarisches-Ranking.2021.98.html (20.07.2012)